Praise f

"Lynn is one of the most profound people of our time. ... shamanistic traditions has provided effective guidance to me and to many others looking for answers. I love her!"

—Dannion Brinkley, author of *Saved by the Light*

Praise for *Medicine Woman*

"One wonders if Carlos Castaneda and Lynn Andrews have not initiated a new genre of contemporary literature: Visionary Autobiography."

—*San Francisco Review of Books*

"First class. . . . A remarkable adventure into the world of the spirit."

—*San Francisco Examiner-Chronicle*

"There is much wisdom here. . . . What sometimes appears as madness may contain its own wisdom; and what may sometimes sound like wisdom may be madness. It is precisely this intricate balance that the medicine woman must learn to keep."

—*Santa Fe Reporter*

"*Medicine Woman* has to do with the meaning of life, the role of women, and the wrestling of power away from the forces of evil that hold it."

—*Los Angeles Times*

"*Medicine Woman* is a well-written, powerful, and exciting tale of the author's apprenticeship with a medicine woman. . . . As in the Castaneda books, it weaves teachings of shamanic philosophy into the telling of the story."

—*Circle*

"Thought-provoking and absorbing."

—*New Woman's Times*

"The revealing story of how women from different cultures view each other and learn from each other."

—Stan Steiner, author of *The New Indians*

"Lynn Andrews celebrates the power of female spirituality. . . . Her dramatic retelling of shamanistic wisdom and ancient Indian philosophy is rich in authentic detail."

—*The Victoria Advocate*

"A fascinating story full of marvelous symbols."

—Books of the Southwest

"A powerful and beautiful story."

—The Guardian, London

"Her story tells and reminds us of ancient wisdoms that we can take with us on our own unique journeys through life no matter what heartfelt path we are on."

—WomanSpirit

"An exciting and insightful story . . . about the interrelatedness of all things."

—The Lammas Little Review

"A statement of what is called for and possible in all of us."

—Sojourner

Praise for *Jaguar Woman*

"Amid primal landscapes, perilous and shimmering between the spirit world and reality, Andrews' narrative opens a window onto an aspect of Native American cultures seldom explored."

—Los Angeles Times

"She speaks of reclaiming her personal powers as a woman. Through a wealth of practical shamanistic lore interwoven with tales of sorcery, Andrews reveals both the challenges and the rewards of the sacred quest."

—New Dimensions Radio Network

Praise for *Star Woman*

"A glimpse of other realities . . . we're reminded once again of the power of our thoughts and the crippling effects of fear and self-limitation."

—San Francisco Chronicle

"A wondrous spiritual and temporal progress as an apprentice medicine woman . . . one woman's quest for spiritual unity and enlightenment."

—Booklist

Praise for *Crystal Woman*

"Undulates with visual hallucinations and other-worldly experiences, but also contains some quite accessible truths about the drama of the human condition."

—*San Francisco Chronicle*

"Full of magic and other-worldly mystery. It reads like fiction and makes you think about how many things there are that we don't know."

—Rona Jaffe, author of *The Best of Everything*

Praise for *Windhorse Woman*

"[Andrews's] Himalayan jaunt is dotted with episodes of crystal power, tears of joy, wise women, rapt visions and talk of healing Mother Earth."

—*Publisher's Weekly*

Praise for *The Woman of Wyrrd*

"Reading like historical romance, this will be snapped up by Andrews's large following."

—*Publisher's Weekly*

"As always, Andrews provides a good, strong story that balances the dramatic with the spiritual. Moreover, Andrews relates a great deal of philosophical thought without excessive commentary. The strength of the teaching forces the reader to greater awareness."

—*Library Journal*

Praise for *Shakkai*

"This New Age narrative, slipping between present and future settings and heavy with symbolism, will please readers who share Andrews's spiritual orientation."

—*Publisher's Weekly*

Praise for *Woman at the Edge of Two Worlds*

"This beautifully and sensitively written book should be a helpful guide to all women going through menopause. It describes the spiritual dimensions of one of the most important transitions in a woman's life. I highly recommend it."

—Susan M. Lark, MD, author of *The Menopause Self-Help Book*

"Lynn Andrews helps every woman find a sense of her own importance."

—Marianne Williamson, author of *A Return to Love* and *A Woman's Worth*

"With this book, Lynn Andrews heals women by reframing our old cultural definition of menopause, which is loss and worthlessness, into one of love, power, wisdom, and most important, self-esteem."

—Alanna E. Tarkington, psychotherapist and author of *Now It's Our Turn*

Praise for *Tree of Dreams*

"Once again Lynn Andrews looks to the Sisterhood of the Shields for guidance and illumination. She places in their hands her vulnerability, and ours, as she reveals the deeper fears and grief of every maturing woman. Her teachers heal her, and they heal us. Lynn Andrews has shared with us her magic once again."

—Marianne Williamson, author of *A Return to Love* and *A Woman's Worth*

"In *Tree of Dreams*, Lynn Andrews speaks candidly from the heart of her personal experience with facing elderhood and death, and in so doing gives us the courage to welcome the lessons of our own experience with these transitions."

—Sarah Edwards, coauthor of *The Practical Dreamer's Handbook*

Praise for *Love and Power*

"With exquisite clarity, *Love and Power* disarms the central complexities of the psyche that drain away (or abort) our access to personal freedom."

—Barbara Hand Clow, author of *The Pleiadian Agenda*

"Lessons of the soul . . . love empowered. What wisdom this wonderful book offers! Lynn explores the secrets for balancing love with power, charting a path to integrate them into our lives. Never has her voice been truer, stronger, or more generous of spirit."

—Hal Zina Bennett, PhD, author of *Write Starts* and *The Lens of Perception*

Praise for *Walk in Balance*

"Lynn Andrews deserves a permanent place of honor among the great teachers who have shared their ever-unfolding knowledge of the sacred mysteries through storytelling. . . . How grateful we should be for such teachers!"

—Hal Zina Bennett, PhD, author of *Write Starts* and *The Lens of Perception*

STAR
WOMAN

Medicine Woman Series
Medicine Woman
Spirit Woman
Jaguar Woman
Star Woman
Crystal Woman
Windhorse Woman
The Woman of Wyrrd
Shakkai
Woman at the Edge of Two Worlds
Dark Sister
Tree of Dreams

Also by Lynn Andrews
Teachings around the Sacred Wheel
The Power Deck
Walk in Balance
Love and Power
Walk in Spirit
Writing Spirit
Coming Full Circle
Sacred Vision Oracle
Acts of Power

LYNN V. ANDREWS
LEGACY LIBRARY

STAR WOMAN

**We Are Made from Stars
and to the Stars We Must Return**

Interior Illustrations by David Tamura

Cover Artwork by Diana Lancaster

BEYOND WORDS
Portland, Oregon

BEYOND WORDS

1750 S.W. Skyline Blvd., Suite 20
Portland, Oregon 97221-2543
503-531-8700 / 503-531-8773 fax
www.beyondword.com

First Beyond Words paperback edition March 2024

Previously published in 1986 by Warner Books, ISBN 978-0-446-51316-6

BEYOND WORDS PUBLISHING and colophon are registered trademarks of Beyond Words Publishing. Beyond Words is an imprint of Simon & Schuster, LLC

For more information about special discounts for bulk purchases, please contact Beyond Words Special Sales at 503-531-8700 or specialsales@beyondword.com.

Managing editor: Lindsay Easterbrooks-Brown
Editor: Michele Ashtiani Cohn & Bailey Potter
Cover Design: Devon T. Smith
Composition: William H. Brunson Typography Services

Manufactured in the United States of America

10 9 8 7 6 5 4 3 2 1

Library of Congress Cataloging-in-Publication Data has cataloged the hardcover edition as follows:

   1. Andrews, Lynn V.   2. Cree Indians—Religion and mythology.   3. Shamans—Biography.   4. Indians of North America—Religion and mythology.   I. Title.
E99.C88A54   1986   299'.78   86-40038

ISBN (hardcover) 978-0-446-51316-6
ISBN (paperback) 978-1-58270-932-1

The corporate mission of Beyond Words Publishing, Inc.: *Inspire to Integrity*

To the memory of my father,
Leif K. Eggers,
who gave me courage

and

To the memory of Georgia O'Keeffe,
a woman of power

This is a true story. Some of the names and places in this book have been changed to protect the privacy of those involved.

Contents

Letter from the Publisher

Dear Reader,

It is a pleasure and an honor to bring you this book from *New York Times* bestselling author Lynn V. Andrews. This book was first published by Lynn in the 1980s as part of a series that has been enjoyed by millions over the years. Lynn was careful to change names and places and sacred ceremonies out of respect for the Indigenous cultures she studied with. For Beyond Words Publishing, it has been a blessing to have known and worked with Lynn over the years and we hope you find her writings as empowering as we do.

With gratitude,
Michele Ashtiani Cohn

Star Woman

In the corner of the forest
where fences begin
Star Woman takes off her clothes
drapes them gently across
galaxies
carefully saying
Night is my serpent
Look in the mirror & dream
She says we are not expected
to know what this means—
Moth flicker on red geraniums
touch of Star during the day
outside the window often
right now

—Jack Crimmins

Introduction

I first met Agnes Whistling Elk eleven years ago. I was an art collector at the time and was very interested in an American Indian marriage basket I had seen in a photography show in Los Angeles. I had a great deal of trouble tracking down the basket, which was shadowed by great mystery. Finally, through a series of bizarre events and magical dreams, I came to believe Agnes had access to the marriage basket. I traveled to the Cree reservation in Manitoba, Canada, where she lived to find out if I could buy it.

What I found instead was a remarkable and compelling woman. "The marriage basket cannot be bought or sold. It can only be earned," she said, watching me with eyes like polished mirrors. She was a full-blooded Cree woman, and her face was creased like that of an apple doll. She was ageless; she could have been fifty or ninety-five. Her cheekbones were high, and she wore her long hair woven in braids that fell well below her shoulders. Around her neck she wore a beaded medicine wheel.

During this first meeting Agnes said to me, "Your life is a path. Knowingly or unknowingly, you have been brought here by a vision quest. It is good to have a vision, a dream."

Agnes spoke with a thick accent that I at first found difficult to understand. At times she had trouble formulating the simplest of thoughts in English, while at other times the most complex ideas would flow with ease. But even when she struggled to articulate her thoughts, she had great dignity.

"Woman is the ultimate," she told me as we sat before an open fire. "Mother Earth belongs to woman, not man. She carries the void."

Agnes Whistling Elk is an Indigenous medicine woman, and since the time of that first meeting I have been her apprentice. She and Ruby Plenty Chiefs, who is also a medicine woman, are my teachers.

At the time Agnes took me on as her student, I asked her if she didn't think it was strange for someone like me from Beverly Hills to be sitting in her quiet cabin in Manitoba asking for help.

"There are always helpers and signs to point the way for anyone who is willing to follow them," she said. "Unknowingly, for the first time in your life, you have followed your true path. No, it is not surprising that you are here. Many omens have spoken of your coming, and I would be bewildered if it were any other way."

Agnes then asked me to write of my experiences with her, to "let the eagles fly" and teach people in an effort to heal our sacred Mother Earth. She said it had been told to her in prophesy that I was to become a warrioress of the rainbow people. She said that one day I would become a bridge between two different worlds, the primal mind and the consciousness of nonindigenous people.

The series of books I am writing are my attempt to fulfill Agnes's instruction by recording the extraordinary adventures and shamanistic teachings I have encountered. These books stress the ancient powers of woman. This ancient knowledge has been memorized and beaded into history by powerful Indigenous women in order to protect and preserve it for continuing life on this beautiful earth. The long-hidden shamanistic society of women that preserves this knowledge is known as the Sisterhood of the Shields. This secret society is based on the ancient traditions of woman and until recently was a circle of women representing only the Indigenous cultures from around the world. Because of the energy changes on our planet, a few women of other races have now been initiated. My own initiation into the society was the culmination of much of my learning with Agnes. Now we of the Sisterhood of the Shields share our knowledge collectively, between tribes and nations, in an attempt to bring balance, wisdom, and a more complete view of truth to the land.

I once asked Agnes what she thought about the biblical expression "Many are called but few are chosen." She laughed and said that we are all called, and we are all chosen if we simply have the courage to step into the unknown. I have written so that you may also share in the ancient traditions as memorized by Agnes Whistling Elk and the Sisterhood of the Shields.

Agnes never tells me what I must learn. She simply puts me into a situation where I must grow and change to survive. In my first book, *Medicine Woman*, I recounted how Agnes guided me through the four aspects of my beginning work. First, she wanted to make me physically strong. Through exposing me to the rigors of her beautiful homeland, its primal forests, raging streams, and unspoiled fields, Agnes brought health and strength to my body. She feels that there must be a balance between what one learns spiritually and physical endurance.

Second, she placed me in situations where I learned to balance the maleness and femaleness within me. A lot of that training had to do with my search for the sacred marriage basket, which culminated in my being pitted against an adept male sorcerer named Red Dog. He had stolen the sacred basket, and to retrieve it I had to undertake a dangerous struggle. To my surprise, I won, although Red Dog and his apprentices Ben and Drum have never ceased to plague me.

Third, Agnes also taught me about making an act of power or an act of beauty in the world. For me, that was writing a book. I learned the reason for an act of beauty is to create a mirror for yourself, so that you can begin to know intimately who you are.

Lastly, Agnes made it clear to me, through paranormal events, my travels in Canada, and my work in dreaming, that a person must be lifted out of her mechanical existence long enough so that real change and transformation has a chance to occur. A space must be created so that our structures and beliefs can be suspended long enough to enable us to hear something new. As a result, during my apprenticeship, I have been able to restructure my orthodox beliefs as to who I am and what the world is around me.

Flight of the Seventh Moon, my second book later retitled *Spirit Woman*, recounted how Agnes initiated me into my ceremonies. She took me around a circle of learning, giving me a working *mandala*, a shield that I can carry in my everyday life. Within the experiences of my rites of passage is the ancient wisdom of woman, and so these lessons culminated with my initiation into the Sisterhood of the Shields. My story is like the story of all women involved in the search. Only our situations are different, because we are all unique. But our source of information is the same. Agnes has always stressed the importance and value of being a woman. She has told me, "Enlightenment is arrived at in a different way for a woman than for a man." When I asked her if she taught men in the same way that she taught women, she laughed and told me to discover that answer for myself. "Teach the next ten men you meet how to have a baby," she said.

In *Jaguar Woman*, my third book in the series, I explored a range of movement similar to that of the butterfly covering this continent in its wanderings from Canada to Mexico. The book describes my lessons of transit, and my meeting with the Sisterhood of the Shields in pursuit of further knowledge and the adventure of the spirit. In the course of this quest, I again traveled north to meet my teachers, Agnes Whistling Elk and Ruby Plenty Chiefs, in Manitoba. But the book did not only explore physical changes of locale; it also examined the process of psychic, mental, and emotional movement from one state of mind to another, and movement from one attribute of perception to another. My experiences took me to the center of the sacred spiral in order to reclaim my original female nature—the real woman within.

Such a journey can only be fully understood in terms of the medicine wheel, which is one of the greatest tools of the early Indigenous people traditions. In teaching, this simple existential paradigm becomes ever more complex; it is a rich and subtle symbol of mystical and philosophical depth. Apprentices are taught to use the medicine wheel as a map to their innermost being. The four directions on the wheel represent categories of introspection and extrospection: the south represents trust and innocence; the west is the home of the sacred dream, death and rebirth; wisdom and strength live in the north; and in the east is illumination.

The key to using the medicine wheel is movement, the way a person moves from one direction to another. For example, a woman living in trust and innocence in the south of the medicine wheel may progress through a series of life experiences and reach a state of wisdom and strength in the north. At this point of wisdom, she has grown from a life of materialism in the south to a position of spirit in the north. The key to evolving further is again movement. Because she has gone from the south looking north for the spirit, she must now move from north in spirit looking south for substance. After manifesting substance, she must then travel back north to manifest spirit, and so on.

I am a woman and a seeker.

Star Woman is a description of the inner visions of one woman in relation to her outward circumstances. It is my fourth book.

I am not an anthropologist, though some persist in casting me in that role. I am interested in wisdom and personal power. Periodically I detach myself from my own culture in search of ancient knowledge. In the process I still live and work closely with my teachers, Agnes Whistling Elk and Ruby Plenty Chiefs, both women of unbelievable force and magnetism.

"Everyone's life is being in a trap," Agnes once said to me. "But this is especially true of women. I am teaching you the ways of an escape artist, how to remove yourself from your own delusions. For a woman there are many predators. I am teaching you more than simply how to run and hide. I am teaching you how to make your stand."

I have tasted something of the mystery and enchantment of Agnes's *Weltanschauung*, a German word that means, literally, "view of the world," but is often translated as "worldview" or "world philosophy." Agnes's shamanistic ideology holds women in a sacred position— indeed, the central position.

During my apprenticeship I have kept careful notes, but I have not been interested in the nomenclature or the order of the anthropological complexities presented to me. I am the apprentice to a medicine woman, not a participant observer. Through initiation I have learned various aspects of a highly secretive set of magical/religious principles and precepts. Through the practice of these traditions of ethnomedicine, I have grown to accept broader metaphysical beliefs than those posited by my own culture.

There are various points of divergence between what I have experienced and what I believe to be rationally possible. As Agnes once pointed out, "There is a chasm between your world and mine. You are trying to make the leap to the other side where I stand. Over here the world is free and magical. Over there you have a millstone around your neck."

Before I met Agnes Whistling Elk and Ruby Plenty Chiefs, I was culture-bound. By that I mean that I led an ordinary life in a large city. I was contained within my cultural milieu. My constructs and values were shaped as a result of normal interaction within this framework.

In one conversation I had with Ruby, who was blinded as a young girl but has learned as a medicine woman to see better than most anyone, she said, "Women need to heal themselves. Do that first in order to heal the men, who need it as much as we do. Remember, only a woman can heal a man spiritually. If you yourself fail, you are two down."

During the course of the experiences I have recorded in *Star Woman*, I was put into a situation by my medicine women and the Sisterhood of the Shields where I met another great teacher, an unexpected one. I established a relationship with Arion, the great white stallion. He was a vehicle for transformation, a shaman transport. Because of the love and trust I felt for him, he was a great mirror for me, with a compelling life of his own. Like a sacred smoke or a drumbeat that magically shifts you into other realms, Arion pulled me into areas where I would not have ordinarily gone. I allowed him to carry me because I totally accepted his power, as a womb accepts the seed of an unborn child.

Agnes once said, "If you become content with your own support group, you limit yourself to walking around in the same familiar circles." Arion propelled me into a shamanistic journey that I could not have traveled on alone. *Star Woman* is a journey through my own fears, the barriers of my consciousness, my self-constructed limitations. To move beyond these barriers is to approach formlessness and the essence from which we are made. This book recounts a journey, at the end of which I traveled beyond the limits of my own form.

A teacher takes you to a fork in the trail, at which point you have a chance to go back over the paths you have walked before or journey into an unknown region. In *Star Woman* there are many forks. At one point I took the familiar path into a fear addiction, and I fell off Arion and was nearly killed. "It's just like I told you. That fear of yours gets you every time," Agnes said as she healed me with her crystals.

This book is about my healing journey on this continent. This work is the fourth in my series, and in a sense, it is a completion book, the end of a circle or "the place where the circle joins itself." When a circle is completed, one simply moves on to other rounds.

For me, the next round is Australia and the Women of the Sacred Dreamtime.

—LVA
Red Deer
Alberta, Canada
August 1985

1

The Ghost Horse

The wind carried an eerie moan, and a full moon had risen above the shadowy spires of pines. The sky was frosted with stars and stabbed by faint shards of color—blue, green, and orange—from the northern lights.

Two bloody tenderloin strips of deer meat hung from forked sticks over the glowing coals of the campfire. The fire spit when juices fell. The three older Indigenous Indian women who surrounded the campfire looked like phantoms in the milky darkness. Their wrinkled faces were fire-scarlet and chiseled with deep shadows. It was cold, and our breath steamed from our noses. Agnes Whistling Elk sat on my left. On my right was July, a young Cree girl in her twenties. Ruby Plenty Chiefs sat next to her. Directly across the fire was a withered old lady with white hair that was uncombed and loose.

July nervously pushed some wild onions and turnips on a flat rock nearer the coals. I, too, felt unnerved by the old woman, whose gaunt eyes never left my face. She had appeared mysteriously and sat down with us, warming herself. I turned to ask Agnes who the old woman was, but the look in her eyes stopped me from speaking.

"Pay attention," Agnes said.

I studied the woman in the light of the fire. I had thought that we were the only people within a hundred miles of the area, and yet here she was, appearing in the midnight hours out of the bush. Her gaze seemed so intent on me that it frightened me, and I began to shiver. Out of desperation, I asked, "Agnes, why did you desert me on the ledge?"

Earlier that evening Agnes and I had hiked up the steep side of a mountain. We had followed a sort of trail where loose rocks slipped from underneath my feet. At the top Agnes told me to sit down on a rock outcropping and watch the vast arroyo hundreds of feet below. She left me while the sky in the west turned crimson.

It was not an unusual experience for me to be sitting alone somewhere hundreds of miles from the nearest outpost of civilization. Agnes had often led me to spots and deserted me. So I made myself as comfortable as I could, slinging off my pack and canteen and trying to derive as much from the situation as possible. Most of the time Agnes gave me explicit directions, but this time she had said nothing. I was just to sit patiently and observe whatever happened.

Darkness was falling, and my first concern was that I would have to hike back to our camp with the aid of a flashlight. The full moon would help considerably. I heard an owl. In the arroyo, ruffled grouse were making their peculiar drumming sound. The wind began to whistle down the draw. After a while I lay on my back. The Milky Way, what Agnes called River Strewn with Rocks, was visible in all its majesty.

The tattoo of horse's hooves broke the silence, and I sat up with a jerk. My most precious dreams and deepest fears all descended on me at once in the raging form of a giant dappled gray stallion. I wondered if I were seeing a ghost. Out of nowhere he charged, the frost of the night glistening on his coat like a diamond mist. He stood pawing the earth at the crest of the mountain. I let out a loud gasp and ran behind a U-shaped boulder. The horse screamed a high-pitched warning as he saw me. The animal threw his legs up, kicking, and then galloped toward me. He reared above me, his silver hooves clattering over the jasper rocks and sending grizzly echoes of bones scraping into the soft night. I jumped out of the way, and he reared again, tossing his magnificent, chiseled head. His thick mane, shadowed red and blue by the moon, rippled like waves of rain in a torrential storm. His being contained power and exquisite beauty. I crouched lower behind a rock in terror and awe, watching this menacing prince of the night tear at the stones to try to reach me.

Suddenly I heard a movement to my left, followed by a low, inquiring whinny. I turned to see one of the stallion's mares; she must have got lost from his herd. Hearing the whinny, the stallion snorted at me. He tossed his head high and, with the first sign of gentleness he had shown, nickered softly. With a bound, he joined his bay filly. He nuzzled her neck, biting her gently, and herded her back toward the shadows of the pines. He stopped for a moment in a spot where he was bathed in moonlight. His front legs were apart and firmly planted. He tossed his head up and down, turned like a silver whirlwind, and disappeared.

I was ashamed to be so frightened, but my heart was racing and I could hardly catch my breath. I thought I had reacted quite calmly under the circumstances, but now I was undone. I did deep breathing for perhaps five minutes. Then I heard a low rumbling, not unlike thunder. At the bottom of the basin, I saw him—my ghost horse. He was about a hundred feet in advance of a herd of wild mustangs. There were more than fifty of them, raising a great cloud of dust as they ran. They were of every color, proud, fierce, and alive. That quality of wildness and aliveness jolted me into the moment. I was completely absorbed—so absorbed that my fright disappeared.

As the memory of that vision faded, I realized Agnes had still not answered me, so I asked her again. "Why did you desert me on the ledge today, Agnes?"

She said, "I left you on the ledge because I knew the horses would not come for me. They were yours. I did not want to spoil it for you."

"What difference did it make whether you were there or not?"

"You journeyed into the wilderness of your own soul, the wildness of your inner landscape. Those horses were for you alone, and I could have waited there forever and never seen them. It was your power that brought them. But be careful; those horses can also trample you."

"I realize that," I said. "I was nearly killed."

Agnes bent forward to cut pieces of the cooked meat for each of us.

We began to eat, but the old woman with hair that looked like a scraggly mane refused the meat Agnes offered her. She was still looking at me, and after a while her gaze pulled my eyes to meet hers. Her gnarled hand reached under her blue shirt and produced a worn horseshoe. She still did not speak. She held the horseshoe to her lower abdomen. Her eyes narrowed, nearly closing. She began to make a soft guttural sound that reminded me of a horse whinnying.

Suddenly she thrust the horseshoe to me over the fire. I thought I smelled burning human flesh, but the woman just held her arm still without showing a sign of pain.

"My name is Twin Dreamers, and I see you from both directions. This horse moccasin is my gift to you from my woman spirit."

I quickly took the horseshoe, terribly worried about her arm. But she seemed unmoved as she returned it to her lap.

"In the ancient way of woman, from far away, the horseshoe was a symbol of your female parts. Now it is a symbol of your new becoming. Whenever you see a white horse, know that the spirit is with you. You need a new mirror in which to see yourself."

I noticed that I could see her reflection on the shiny surface of the horseshoe, which was highly polished.

"You will soon discover a new teacher—one who rides between many worlds. You are approaching the last giveaway in this circle of teaching. Listen to the winds—they tell the legends of the galaxies. To learn of the stars, you must burn like they do. In time this will come to pass. In time your new teacher will prepare you for your journey to the stars. Only then can you complete this circle and go on to teach your people where they come from and what they are made of."

"Ho," I said. "I have eaten. I am full." I held the horseshoe to my heart.

Twin Dreamers moved back from the fire. Her face was soon taken by the outer darkness, and she disappeared into the night.

2

Shape-Shifter

Back home in Southern California a week later, I decided to take a vacation and drive up the coast to the Santa Barbara Horse Show with my daughter, Vanessa. She very much wanted me to go and to bring her horse in a trailer with us. We thoroughly enjoyed our chance to be alone.

We were on the freeway early. Vanessa kept turning around to look through the rear window at the trailer we were pulling behind the pickup. Then she would look quickly back at the traffic. I could see she was excited. At eighteen, Vanessa had bright blue eyes and thick blond hair like the mane of a lion. The pink-and-white oleander bushes were vibrantly in bloom, and the salt air wafted in through the truck windows in soft billowing gusts.

I surely deserved this long overdue rest. I had gone through so many ceremonies in the world of magic, and I had been writing books for what seemed like eons. I had been in constant confrontations with what Agnes called the *heava* side of the spirit or, in psychological terms, the dark side of the personality. Again and again I had walked or bungled my way through one fear after another. I had found triumph and joy in watching the reflected painting of my own being, but today I felt far from Canada and the Maya jungles. I just wanted to enjoy my daughter and indulge in my intense love for the equine spirit—the indomitable horse.

We found our stall at the show grounds and parked nearby.

"It's three hours until your jumping class," I said, after looking at my watch.

Vanessa was elated. "I'll go get my number and register, Mom."

I watched her disappear into the crowd of people and horses. I put a lead on Shahzonn, our horse, and led him out of the trailer. He snorted and rolled his eyes but soon calmed as I acquainted him with the new surroundings by walking him around for a little while. Shah is a fifteen-hands-high Arabian who looks small and fine-boned in comparison to the larger Thoroughbred jumpers. People turned up their noses at him, and I chuckled to myself. Never had I seen a horse more skilled at or more eager to jump than Shahzonn. Still a colt at five years old, beautiful and graceful like a gazelle, he burned hot and wild with the deserts of Egypt in his soul. He was uneasy from the blaring loudspeakers calling classes and the crush of riders and grooms. I led him over to his stall, where I began to prepare him for the ring. I had decided to drive up from Los Angeles without a trainer or groom. Though less professional, the three of us would have more fun on our own.

I cross-tied Shahzonn and began polishing his hooves. I closed the stall doors in hopes of calming him down. Shah's behavior was decidedly erratic, but I finished preparing him with show sheen on his coat and a last-minute clipping. Vanessa came in, put on her riding habit, and soon went out to the truck to put her hair up under her hard hat. As she closed the stall door, I turned around to face Shah. He peered at me oddly for several moments and then slowly stretched his nose to mine. His breath was hot on my cheek, and he took in my own breath slowly and deliberately. He had never done any such thing before. I stepped back a pace. Shah let out a high, piercing whistle, and his body shivered, taking on a peculiar phosphorescent color. He reared up straight into the air, snapping his ties off the halter. His belly contracted and expanded and then seemed to fill up with light. It was covered with shimmering blue, green, yellow, and pink rainbows, incomprehensibly shining through his skin like the aurora borealis of the far north. The rays streaked and splashed through the stall, seeming to push at me. I slipped and fell backward against the door just as Vanessa opened it. She caught me in her arms.

"Mom, what on earth is happening? I'm the one who's supposed to be nervous and fainting."

I got up, brushing the shavings off my jeans.

"What was that strange-looking old Indian lady doing in here?" Vanessa asked. She petted Shah, who was now very docile and ordinary.

"What woman are you talking about?"

"Well, some woman just walked out of this stall."

"There was no woman." I looked out the door of the stall and saw no one except a young girl on a horse. I tried to center myself and catch my breath. Vanessa was staring at me, shaking her head in an expression of puzzlement. "Look, I must have a case of show nerves," I said, shaking my head and carefully examining Shah's eyes. They were the same brown eyes but had a slight film over them. I saw no expression or sign of recognition. I felt a tingling up my spine and knew my vacation was over.

"Vanessa, come on. You only have twenty minutes," I said after looking at my watch.

"Okay, okay. How do I look?"

"Perfect." I gave the English saddle one last swipe with the cleaning cloth, and we walked Shah out into the sunlight. His gray coat glistened over his rippling muscles. I gave Vanessa a knee up, and she rode over to the warm-up ring, which was thronged with other young riders all preparing for open jumping. They trotted and cantered, and a few took low jumps. I leaned against the rail, watching. My heart pounded as I observed Shahzonn. I wondered what had happened in the stall and why he now looked so spiritless. He was shuffling around the ring instead of lifting his legs high, and he was holding his tail low, not arched as usual. I motioned for Vanessa to ride over. I felt Shah's muzzle and stroked his neck. He seemed fine, but certainly different.

"What's wrong, Mom?"

The loudspeaker blared the announcement of open jumping for those eighteen years and younger.

"Does Shah seem okay to you, Vanessa?"

"Yeah, fine. He's really collected."

"Well, he just seemed like maybe he didn't feel well."

"Mother," Vanessa said, stretching out the word. "Just relax." She winked at me. "I have to go. I'm second up, and I want to watch Jessie's Chance go around the course."

"Good luck, sweetheart. Have fun."

I felt such pride in my daughter as I watched her take her place as a young woman. She rode with great courage and assurance. Soon I joined the swarm of onlookers in the bleachers of the main arena. I was emotionally charged. Jessie's Chance knocked down one pole going over the brick wall—not a great score.

Vanessa's number was called. "Number 117," croaked the announcer. "Riding Shahzonn is Vanessa Andrews, a fine young equestrian from Southern California. This little gray is one of the few Arabians in jumping today. Let's give her a hand."

Horse and rider cantered into the ring, circled around, and started for the first jump. They moved as one. Shah took the first jump effortlessly and the next in and out, then moved on to the water jumps. As they approached the stone wall, which was four feet high, they galloped right by where I sat. I could not help but remember Shahzonn's wild eyes and the colors shining through his belly like Christmas tree lights. What could possibly have happened in those moments in the stall? Shah's eyes now seemed lusterless, and he behaved like a gentle cow pony. Arabian horses are hot-blooded and highly spirited. Yet Shah was performing as if by rote—perfectly, but without sparkle. When he jumped, he usually owned the ring. He would perform like a star playing to the camera. But today he simply ran a perfect course. Vanessa was thrilled, but I could not help but wonder what was going on.

I was standing at the horse entrance to the arena after all the other horses and riders had received their ribbons. Vanessa cantered into the ring. Shahzonn appeared sleepy as my daughter received her trophy. The crowd in the stands clapped and cheered. The photographer's popping flashbulbs did not seem to startle Shah.

"That horse doesn't act like an Arab," someone said. The voice was familiar and directly behind me.

Another voice I recognized said, "Yeah, that horse acts like a push-button fifteen-year-old Thoroughbred. Some Arabian."

I turned around irritably. Standing before me, wearing jeans, Stetsons, fitted cowboy shirts, and expensive cowboy boots, were Ben and Drum, whom I had known as Red Dog's apprentices and who were usually not far from their teacher. I was shocked and glanced around suspiciously for any sign of Red Dog, the sorcerer who had figured so prominently in my past. As a neophyte medicine woman, I had come up against Red Dog's evil genius more than once.

"Don't worry," Drum said, seeing my concern. "Me and Ben have left sorcery forever."

"You bet," Ben agreed.

"What are you doing here?" I asked, reluctant to believe a word they said.

Just then the ring announcer called, "Gate, please." Ben and Drum hustled the gate closed behind the next class of riders. Vanessa, still mounted on Shahzonn, waved at me from twenty yards away.

Drum came back over, followed by Ben. "Yeah, we met a guy out of Billings, Montana," Drum said. "Raises rodeo stock mostly. Doing some other stuff too. Cross-breeding some interesting animals."

"How did you meet him?"

"After what you and Jaguar Woman did to me in the Yucatan, I couldn't handle sorcery anymore. Red Dog was humiliated and became more and more evil after you and your women took his jaguar mask."

"One of the lowest acts a sorcerer can perform is to steal another shaman's face or mask. We tricked you and Red Dog so we could return the jaguar mask to its rightful owner. Red Dog blatantly stole it, if you recall. Red Dog deserved to lose his dignity. He misused his power," I said, glaring at Drum.

He immediately realized his error and almost jumped backward. He had all but betrayed me into the hands of Red Dog in the jungles of Mexico. I had been a blundering fool, but his act had been treacherous.

"Yes. Oh, yes. You're right. It was all a big mistake," Drum said.

"So you're out of the sorcery game now, are you?"

"Yeah," Ben chimed in. "Now we're rodeoing full-time."

"Looks like it." I indicated the gate, sarcastically.

"Well, we're just ring attendants right now, picking up a few bucks before we work our way up to Sacramento."

"We're riding broncs up there and helping the guy we met," Drum added hurriedly. "Hey, listen. No hard feelings about what happened. You're right; the mask didn't belong to Red Dog. Your woman's circle showed us good. You beat Red Dog again."

I frowned, recalling Drum's mischief.

"Hey, Red Dog made me do all that," Drum insisted. "I didn't really want to do that stuff. Red Dog had control of me. I had no choice. What would you do if Agnes or Ruby told you to do something?"

I shook my head in disgust.

Drum dug his needle-nosed boot tip into the dirt. "Neat belt buckle," he said nervously. He pointed to his midsection. The silver buckle had come from the Calgary Stampede. "I won it in bronc riding—fifth time out."

I turned away. "What happened to you, Ben? I thought you were in Oklahoma looking for that power man named David Carson. Did you ever find him?"

"Yeah, I found him all right. Cursed be the day I was born. He lived in a little shack on the Kiamichi River near a town, if you want to call it that, called Tuskahoma."

"Well, what happened?" I prodded.

"It was hell. Full of insects farmers call 'chiggers.' And snakes. I even saw an alligator right by my foot. Well, anyway, I got there at night. I was all scraped with brambles and half eaten by mosquitoes. Carson came to the door and stuck a shotgun between my eyes and said 'Git!'

"If only I had listened to him! 'But I'm here for teaching,' I managed to stammer. 'I've brought you medicine tobacco and a blanket and a leather wallet that I made myself.' He put his shotgun away and said, 'Let's see.' I handed him the goods real formally. All he was interested in was if there was any money in the wallet. When he saw there wasn't, he got furious and threw it against the wall. Then all of a sudden he turns back to me and he's just as polite and kind as you can imagine. 'Sit down,' he said. 'And take a load off. Where are you from anyway?' I told him I was from Canada. 'I was just getting ready to eat. You hungry?' I told him I honestly hadn't eaten for two days. Well, we had some of the best food I've ever tasted: beaver tail soup, frog legs, catfish, vine-ripened tomatoes, and blackberries as big as your fist for dessert. Purely delicious. I knew right then that Carson was the man to teach me. As if reading my mind, Carson started asking me questions. What did I know about this and what did I know about that? Then he told me that I didn't know much, but he would take me on as an apprentice. He said that most of his apprentices had done fairly well for themselves.

"Then he said, 'What kind of magic are you interested in?' I said I wanted to be a power guy like him and Red Dog. Carson started laughing and fell on the floor holding his stomach. He laughed so hard, he cried. You can imagine how I felt then. When he got up and collected himself, he said, 'You've got to begin somewhere. Earth, air, fire, or water—which one?' I thought about it and chose earth. Carson seemed pleased. 'That's a deep subject,' he said. 'We'll begin in the morning. You can sleep on the couch. Most of the stuffing's out, but it's good enough.'

"The next morning he rolled me out of bed with the birds. 'Earth magic it is,' he said. 'Follow me.' I followed him outside and he handed me a shovel. With the heel of his boot, he traced a circle over the ground. Then he pointed and said, 'Eight—no, make it nine feet deep.'

"That was the hardest digging ground I had ever seen. It was like digging through granite. The hot sun beat down on me. Every once in a while Carson would come and inspect my work. 'Earth magic,' he would say, to encourage me. I worked for ten days on that hole, and then he told me to carry the mound of earth in buckets and throw it in the river. That took me another three days. When that was done, I went and got Carson and told him I was ready to learn earth magic. He said, 'First build an outhouse over the hole.'"

I let out a convulsive laugh. Ben looked as if I had wounded his pride.

"Go on, Ben," I said. "What happened? I don't mean to upset you. But it is funny."

"Well, one night Carson was sitting down while I was washing the jelly jars he called dishes. He thought he saw a shadow under his front door. He didn't bother to look. He just took his shotgun and blew the door off the hinges. No one was there, thankfully. He went back to sipping his white lightning and he told me to fix the door.

"That damned sorcerer! He did some things to me I don't want anyone to ever know about. I was lucky to get out of there with my life."

Ben looked as if he were about to cry. I surveyed both him and Drum and chuckled. The last time I had seen Ben was in the outback of Canada. The last time I had seen Drum was during a ceremony in the jungles of Mexico. I wondered if there was more than chance at work because our paths continually crossed and not always under the best of circumstances.

Vanessa rode up, and I congratulated her. I told her then to go and wait for me in the barn. Ben and Drum were leering at her and continued to do so as she rode off. That distressed me.

"Tell me more about David Carson," I said to Ben.

The name jolted him. Drum also pulled his eyes off my daughter.

"I never want to see him or hear his name again if I can help it. He was worse than Red Dog and Ruby put together."

The announcer called for a lunch break. "Show to resume in one hour," he called over the loudspeaker.

Great tractors came in, pulling implements to grade the show ring flat and free from ruts. Ben continued to complain about the injustices he had suffered at the hands of David Carson as we walked to the hot dog stand. Ben and Drum ordered three hot dogs each and a vast array of other junk food. I ordered hot dogs and drinks for myself and Vanessa. Ben and Drum were full of praise for the cuisine and ate ravenously. I excused myself and left to join Vanessa. She was washing Shahzonn proudly, cracking jokes with two girlfriends who had joined her.

"Mom, who were those weirdos you were talking to?"

I smiled and gave her a big hug. "Honey, it's a long story. Here's a hot dog and a Coke. I'll be back in, what, forty-five minutes?"

"That's fine, Mom." Vanessa and the two girls giggled. Shahzonn was making bizarre faces while sucking water out of the hose.

"Goodbye, Mrs. Andrews," the two girls chirped.

I rejoined Ben and Drum, who were stretched out on the grass, lazing in the sun. I sat next to them under the shade of a willow tree. Ben looked up from making a Bull Durham cigarette. "You know, you really ought to go by and see Doris and Jake Hawks-Above next time you go up to Canada. They live pretty close to Billings."

"Why should I do that, Ben?"

"Well, Jake's a mix of Indian and German or something foreign like that. He raises rodeo stock off the reservation north of Crow Agency."

"I'm not really interested in that kind of thing, Ben."

"You might be real interested in something else he's raising, though. He has these Lippizaners and some big white Andalusian breed that looks like a big Arab." He drew out the word. "He's raising them secretly, trying to perfect a new breed, I think."

"Now, that really does sound interesting," I said, warming to the idea. I wasn't very familiar with the Andalusian breed he described.

"Well, you've never seen horses that are more beautiful. I promise you that."

Ben had finally succeeded in intriguing me. "That does sound unusual. Will they be home in two weeks? I'm flying up to see Agnes, and I could stop by Billings, I guess."

"Well, write him and tell him you're coming. I'll mention it to him myself." He fumbled in his jeans pocket for the stub of a broken pencil and scrawled out the address in practically illegible letters. "Here's his address. Don't miss him, Lynn. It's a real experience."

There was a long silence that was finally interrupted by the announcer calling the first afternoon class. Before parting we walked along together to the gates. I commented on what a surprise it had been to see them at a horse show in Santa Barbara. It was odd meeting in such an offbeat place.

"Maybe it's . . . What's the word, Ben?"

"Karma," Ben said.

"Maybe it's karma," Drum said.

I laughed and said, "Maybe it is."

Vanessa and I left soon after, trailering Shahzonn. We enjoyed a lovely evening drive back to Los Angeles.

3

Horse Maze

I sat in my living room and wrote a short letter to Jake Hawks-Above. I asked if I could visit him and see his horses, then gave him my flight number and arrival time in Billings.

A little more than a week later I received the following reply, written in longhand:

Dear Ms. Andrews,

I don't usually allow visitors, but since I've talked to Ben and Drum and they are friends, I'll let you in to see my stock.

I'm sorry I can't pick you up at the airport myself, but I am sending one of the hands since we have to pick up feed that day anyway.

His name is Axel, and he will be waiting for you when your flight gets in. I will be able to drive you back to the Billings airport when you want.

Yours truly,
Jake Hawks-Above

My usual curiosity had got the better of me, and I tried to find out something more about Hawks-Above and his horses. But I found no reference to him in any horse magazine, and no one I asked seemed to know anything about him. Nevertheless, I made up my mind to go and see these lively animals that Ben had described with such passion. My intentions set, I confirmed my reservations to Alberta, Canada, with a short layover in Billings.

Billings was larger than I had expected, and the airport was situated high on a rimrock that bordered the north edge of town. The downtown area seemed to be southeast of the airport.

"You Lynn?" a grungy cowboy greeted me as I was coming out of the gate with my flight bag. He was just as faded-looking and weathered as his jeans.

"I sure am," I said, shaking his hand.

"Axel here," he drawled. "Let's get going. Still got to fetch some A&M at the feed store."

I waited for him as he got into his old red pickup. As he backed up the truck, it belched great billows of dark-colored smoke. I got in, and we took off recklessly. The engine sounded as if it had a few defects and needed help from a competent mechanic. Axel paid no attention to the sick, coughing motor. He reached inside his Levi's jacket and extracted a pint bottle of whiskey. He took a long pull and then passed it my way.

"Swig?" he asked.

"No, thank you." I grabbed onto the door handle and began praying I would reach my destination in one piece.

"Don't blame you. It's some cheap hooch anyway."

"You think it's safe," I asked, "to drink and try to operate a vehicle?"

"Safe? Hell, I've had fifteen or twenty wrecks when I'm sober. Ain't never had one when I'm drinking."

"I could drive, if you like."

"Honey, I've made it a rule—never get in a truck with a woman driver." He popped the clutch, dropping to a lower gear, and pulled around a string of traffic, barely avoiding a head-on collision before getting back into the right lane.

"Tell me about your boss, Hawks-Above," I said, hoping to distract him from taking any more chances with our lives.

"Him? Nutty as a squirrel. Loves that damned breeding stock. He thinks more of them horses than he does of his help."

Axel hit the brakes suddenly, and I caught myself before flying through the windshield and landing on the hood.

"Sorry," he said. "Didn't know the light was going to change. Damn red lights anyway. They have a way of scaring a man. Stop signs are way better. You can run them."

We miraculously arrived at the feed store and parked with the rear of the pickup bed on the loading docks.

"Won't be a minute," Axel said. "Just have to load up right quick."

"I think I'll get out and stretch my legs," I said.

"Better let me open the door for you, then," Axel said. "Falls off sometimes. Tried to get it welded on, but I took it to a bunch of incompetents."

Axel came around and opened my door, which made a sound like someone stepping on a cat's tail. I did a couple of circles around the gravel parking lot of the feed store while Axel went into the office. Behind the glass, I saw him upending his bottle with the man inside.

"Give me a break," I said, and got back into the truck.

A couple of minutes later two men started pitching sacks of feed into the truck bed. Each time a bag hit, it made me feel like a yo-yo bouncing up and down.

I was beginning to regret my Billings sojourn when Axel got in hurriedly. We took off at breakneck speed, throwing gravel and belching smoke.

"Sumbitch wanted me to pay him," he said. "The nerve of some of these operators. Act like all you're supposed to do is shell out money to them. Hell, we got credit."

Axel was a speed demon. I couldn't believe the truck could go so fast. We were soon on the highway, headed east out of Billings.

We crossed the Yellowstone River before long, the houses thinning along the roadside. The land flattened out into sage-covered prairie. We stopped in Hardin for gas, which Axel pumped. He paid and got a chaser of soda pop, as he called it. On the outskirts of town he said, "Hand me that pint out of the glove box, honey." I did, and every few miles he would take a drink, set the bottle between his legs, and then have a sip of pop.

I asked him about the range of mountains in the distance.

"Those are the Big Horns, honey. They say there's some Indian women still live up there today, been there ever since the Custer massacre. They say those women can make it rain rocks right out of the sky. I believe 'em, too, because I got right in the middle of one of those rock storms one time when I was up there hunting. Damnedest thing you ever saw, just like hail, exceptin' it was stones."

"What did you do?" I asked. "To protect yourself, I mean."

"Hell, I crawled in a hollow log right nearby. If'n I didn't, I reckon I'd be dingier than I am right now."

We turned off east onto a dirt road, the truck sounding like a World War II Messerschmitt. Axel didn't slow down one bit. We were throwing rooster tails of dust, and the oil smoke was still billowing. We started gaining elevation, and the higher we got, the more trees were visible.

"You part Native, Axel?" I inquired.

"Hell, no. I'm a white man, honey. I was raised up around the Indians, though. I know better than to disrespect their ways. Some of them Indians are witches. You get one of them angry at you and you might as well send your saddle home and padlock the barn. That happened to old Sam Hey-man. He stumbled on some Indian doings, and he told them he thought they was a bunch of superstitious morons. Wasn't four days later old Sam was crazier than a bedbug. He said some old chief's ghost was following him around calling him a superstitious moron. Family, doctors, nobody could do anything for him. Finally put old Sam away in the state hospital in Deer Springs."

We veered off the dirt road onto a long gravel driveway lined with tall pine trees on both sides. I saw a sign that said HAWKS-ABOVE. The ranch was ahead of us in a forest. A chain of snow-capped mountains loomed in the distance. We turned right and drove alongside a high, solid brown-board wall that seemed to encompass acres of property. The heavily forested area surrounding the ranch was dark, only a few somber rays of sunlight struggling through the dense foliage. Axel pulled the truck to a stop.

"I'm going to let you out here, honey, and go around to the stock entrance. Just ring the bell over there. Somebody will fetch you."

"Thanks so much, Axel. It's been . . . well, interesting."

I got out, my legs a bit rubbery. Axel drove off hastily. Near the gate was a miniature church bell. I pulled the chain and rang it several times. I felt rather foolish standing there with my flight bag, my hand clasped around the chain that pulled the clapper. I waited and rang it again.

The huge gate started to creak open slowly. A tall, dark man peered around the edge, squinting his tiny eyes. He appeared to be in his sixties and wore his gray hair in a crew cut.

"You the Andrews lady?" he asked severely.

"Lynn, yes . . . sir." I assumed this must be Jake.

"Well it's a good thing you wrote, because I would have never let you in. Rules are that anyone gets caught snoopin' around here gets shot. C'mon, we'll be feeding in just a little while."

I went through the gate, which he then closed and locked with a padlock. I followed him down a path that was well kept, with giant pines and a few aspens growing on either side. At this higher altitude there was a chill in the air, and I was glad I had brought a sweater. The first horse corrals that we came to were populated by mixed-breed horses.

"Rodeo stock," Jake said.

There was a sadness about these horses, as if their fierceness did not come from their innate wildness. A chestnut gelding reached over the fence toward us with an inquiring gaze. Jake doubled his fist and punched him firmly on the nose.

"Get your head back in there," he growled. He turned to me and explained curtly, "Got to teach them who's boss."

The horse reared back and snorted several times. I flinched and decided I could not stand this man, whoever he was. I pulled my sweater around my shoulders as a cold breeze kicked up. Striding along with this eccentric, I felt cold and uneasy. When we rounded a blind corner, though, I gasped and almost forgot my companion. About thirty yards ahead was a black stallion. I blinked to make sure my eyes were not deceiving me. I had never seen such a perfectly formed animal. A diminutive woman held the stud chain on the dancing creature. His eyes were fiery with flecks of red, and he scanned me like a black panther finding his prey. He had a flawlessly dished Arabian head, small for his body, with a heavy, arched neck like the Lippizaners from the Spanish Riding School in Austria. He was fine boned, but in general larger than the usual Arabian. He carried his head and tail high and whinnied as Jake and I approached.

Jake grabbed the stud chain and gave it a sharp tug. The stallion shivered all over and stood at attention, not moving. Jake neglected to introduce the woman, so I extended my hand and introduced myself.

"I'm Doris Hawks-Above," she said in a small voice, peering down at the sandy path. My heart immediately went out to her.

Good grief, I thought. *This is going to be strange.*

Jake began to explain about his secret breeding program. Without giving any details, he told me he was basically crossing the original Bedouin Arabian bloodlines with a wild Andalusian strain found only on the steppes of Russia. I had never heard of any horses like the ones he described being in Russia, but I listened attentively. I ran my hands over the firm muscles of the stallion. He quivered when I pressed in certain places, and I could tell as a healer that he had a lot of pain in his body.

I started to mention this fact but was immediately cut off by an intense scowl from Jake. Doris turned away. Her face held an awesome beauty. She must have been fifty, but she had the clear skin of someone twenty-five. She acted as if she had surrendered her soul to Jake and mirrored his evil with her own goodness. Maybe evil was too strong a word, but it certainly seemed that he was wicked.

"Your bloodlines are producing an extraordinary animal, Jake," I said.

"Yes, they are near perfect. Not quite yet."

"When will you show those horses, and in what way?"

"When the breed reproduces perfectly and shows a consistently high intelligence. Then they will be dressage horses like the Lippizaners or Trakehners."

"How does a rodeo man come to breed such magnificent animals?"

"There is much magic in great beauty," Jake said, his eyes suddenly seeming to leer at me as if I were naked. Then he ran his hands sensually over the neck and shoulders of the back, slowly caressing the horse. A cold gust of north wind swept over my shoulders and turned the aspens into an applause of quaking, vibrating silver.

Jake turned on his booted heel and led the prancing black stallion toward a low-hanging barn with high doors. I noticed that none of the horses in that barn could see out of their stalls.

"Come this way," Doris said. She motioned toward another narrow path between two corrals. The fencing was a mixture of wood and wire. The fading sun ran golden and crimson along the smooth wires, making them look like the veins of a giant living organism. We were walking through the tight labyrinth of one corral made up of one set of stalls after another. Each stall and corral was filled with brood mares, colts, fillies, and stallions. I noticed that the animals were cared for in a natural way, as if in the wild. Some of the horses had hooves that curled up, and none had shoes. Their manes, long and heavy, hung matted and tangled. Their eyes rolled and their heads were constantly moving. It was a living maze with a small dark house in the center that was the providing heart. Doris and I walked around corner after corner. After a while I realized with a shock that there was no way I could find my way out of this giant, breathing labyrinth.

"Why are the stall doors so high?" I asked Doris.

"Because in winter we let the manure pile up and up until finally the horses can see out. The manure provides warmth in sub-zero weather."

"Oh."

There was a high-pitched neighing. We were standing at the entrance of a large enclosure bordered by dark walls. Silhouetted in startling titanium brilliance, a large white stallion reared and bucked. His huge eyes were like fishbowls holding exotic creatures of serpentine colors.

I gasped, and Doris said, "It's okay."

From across the enclosure, I heard another shrill cry that sounded to me like a challenge. From a second gate another white stallion similar to the first reared and snorted. He galloped into the corral, his eyes wild.

"They'll kill each other," I stammered, thinking a horrible error had been made penning them up together.

"Oh, no, they're brothers," Doris said. "They're just greeting each other."

I watched from a distance. The two horses charged each other but stopped short of meeting. I noted that they were virtually identical. They reared and pawed the air, biting and frothing at each other. But never did they actually try to harm each other. They strutted and galloped at runaway speed over the black earth. Their matted forelocks tumbled down to the tips of their noses. Their giant crested necks were like crowns of glory. Their beauty left me speechless. The world could have dropped away, and I would not have known it. How I longed to ride them, like that strong wind that had come up again from the north.

Doris was carefully watching me. I turned to her, smiling. She started to speak but evidently thought better of it. She looked as if she were almost trying to warn me of something. Then Jake appeared and yelled at her to open the gate. As she did so, the stallions charged obediently out of the ring and into waiting stalls. With the horses gone, the ring was completely void of life force. I had the feeling of watching death, witnessing the life and animation of a body go slack as the spirit leaves its host forever. I was having certain misgivings, feeling rising anxiety. I wanted this Jake Hawks-Above to take me back to the

Billings airport as he had promised in the letter. I jumped at the sound of his voice. He had come up silently from behind.

"Come, you must see the breeding charts. They are fascinating." As if reading my thoughts, he added, "Afterward, I will drive you back to Billings." His eyes were so small I couldn't even tell what color they were.

The inside of Doris and Jake's home was small but perfectly neat and clean. Hanging from the log rafters of the cabinlike structure were hundreds and hundreds of Native American artifacts: forty or fifty antique beaded pipe bags and pipes, peyote fans, buffalo robes, parfleches, drums of every size and design, bear traps, arrows and bows, rattles by the hundreds, and dozens and dozens of medicine, tribal, and personal bundles. Beautiful Navajo rugs covered every inch of floor space, and glowing coals from a dying fire burnt in the stone fireplace. We sat in three rocking chairs by the hearth. Doris left for a moment and lit several lanterns, spacing them around the room. Then she joined us and set some chokecherry wine and three glasses on a square pine-tree trunk that stood between us.

"You have no electricity," I remarked.

"Don't like it," Jake said, his tone abrasive. He raised his glass and took a healthy drink of wine, indicating that it would be rude if I did not do the same. I joined him, and Doris also lifted her glass.

"I'm in total awe of your beautiful stallions," I began carefully.

"Yes, yes," Jake said, nodding his head. "But what do you think?"

"Well . . . ah, what do you mean?"

"Did you see the fiends in their eyes? Did you see the wickedness of their natures and spirits?" His voice rose higher. "Did you see my horses?"

I answered softly. "Yes, I did see their wildness."

Ignoring me, he said, "No, you didn't see anything, or you would know that the spirit of the archfiend is in them." Then he shook his head and said, "Don't you wonder why I'm doing all this breeding of horses, particularly these demonic horses?"

There was something terribly wrong with this man. I kept my tone even as I answered him. "Yes, I do."

"Come, let me show you the breeding charts." He stood.

I rose, but Doris remained seated, staring into the fire's embers. I followed Jake into his office. He hung a glowing lamp on a nail, then closed the door. I thought it was strange that he locked it. Against one wall there was a long Spanish desk. Four horse skulls hung above it.

"I've been breeding horses for forty years, and these are the skulls of my first breeding stallions."

The entire room was extraordinary. Every inch of wall and rafter was hung with bones, hanks of hair, skins, herb bundles, and grotesque things I did not recognize. Jake lit two black tapers, and I gasped when I saw a human skull was between them. The skull had a grimly fascinating smile and sat on a black cloth that covered a low altar. Different precious metals and jewels had been attached to the bone surface. The jewels flashed in the flickering candlelight, dimmed, and then flashed again. I wondered if he used the skull in some ritualistic way. I shivered, staring at the awesome trophy.

Jake laughed. "That is the skull of my great teacher. He was Austrian. When I went to Vienna in search of fine horses, I met this great mystic and became his student. His initials were H.M. A teacher's name is not important, only the wisdom he imparts. As I am dedicated to finding the perfect breed of horse, he was breeding the perfect race of man. This was before the war. He went to Nepal, and I studied with him there for many years."

Silent, watching him, I was feeling very awkward and uncomfortable and perhaps even cringing. Perfect race of man and horses, indeed, I thought. "What about the magnificence of life force itself?" I said.

"Hah," he bellowed, his voice rising. "Undirected, it only produces a race of less intelligent mutants." He turned abruptly and went to his desk. He started pulling out drawer after drawer of his chart chest. He waved sheaves of paper in my face, showing me one bloodline chart after another. His small, dark eyes took on a crazy glow as he pontificated about frozen semen from stallions long dead and genes crossing with genes until I couldn't follow his reasoning at all.

"I am going to breed the master horse," he said excitedly. "A horse with paranormal powers so far above the common horse, he will be a god. My master failed with humans, but I will succeed with horses."

"Why is it so important?"

"It is important because I will die. But my creation will live on as a monument to my teacher. I have very nearly succeeded. I would like to show you my masterpiece."

"I'd like to see it."

"Then, we will drink a toast to the spirit of the horse. We will drink from my teacher's skull, first me and then you. Yes, if you are daring enough, we will drink from the brain cavity where the most highly complex matter in the known universe once resided, the locus of cognition for one of the earth's rare geniuses."

The skull seemed to be smiling, and the jewel-encrusted bone sparkled brilliantly from the light of the candle flames. My hand was trembling as I covered my mouth to choke back a gasp.

"You want me to drink from that?" I asked incredulously.

"Yes, in honor of the perfected species and all things known and unknown. I don't want to force you, but if you refuse, you will never see one of the great marvels of our time. I will pour."

Jake took a large hand-blown bottle from underneath his altar. The top of the skull flipped back on a hinge, and he poured in a sanguine-colored liquid. He lifted the skull in a toast and then drank the liquid down. He poured again and handed me the skull. I took it with my thumbs in the eye sockets. I didn't know what else to do, so I drank a swallow. The wine was sweet and tasted like Japanese plum wine. I hurriedly returned the skull to Jake. He laughed in a long, derisive, deep-throated tone that turned into a howl.

I was mesmerized, and I sensed that my very life was suddenly in jeopardy. I began to feel physically strange. The corona around the candle flame seemed to grow larger. I looked across the room at two flat, hazy images. They were tables, but for a moment I had seen them as shields.

"Just a little precaution," Jake said, eyeing me carefully. "I learned all about the concoction you just drank when I was in Nepal. It's harmless, really. But it produces the most wonderful, sometimes the most terrible, dreams."

I was looking around to try to find something with which to protect myself. I saw nothing but a large bone. As a weapon, it struck me as rather ludicrous.

Jake went on. "Ben and Drum told me you are a friend of an old associate of mine."

His words seemed covered with spiny thorns, and I did not want to touch them. I wanted to run.

He continued. "So I took the liberty of inviting him here. He's here now, in fact. I believe you know each other."

A door next to the altar opened and I nearly fainted. There stood Red Dog. He was dressed all in black—black jeans, black ostrich boots, and a black embroidered cowboy shirt with silver tips on the collar. His red beard and hair were unkempt, as usual, and he literally sneered at me with what seemed to be great delight. For several moments we stood staring at each other. My blood felt as if it were running out through the bottoms of my feet and down into the floor. Jake was laughing wildly somewhere in the background. My only thought was *God, how could I have been so stupid as to fall into this one?* This was it. Agnes had said, "Know your death." Well, here it was. I was speechless, either from the effects of the drugged wine or from terror. I did not know which.

To make matters even worse, Ben and Drum appeared beside Red Dog. They were both smiling in contempt.

Red Dog said with finality, "Your vulnerability is your great shield, but it is also your great stupidity. You were the cause of my loss of power and my greatest embarrassment as a sorcerer. If you didn't have the Sisterhood of the Shields behind you, you'd be nothing. Even they don't know what to do with the jaguar mask. How tragic that it is in the inferior hands of women. With their help in the Yucatan, you tricked me out of the mask that should be mine! But this time I will drink out of your skull."

The room was taking on a redness. Although I knew my execution was imminent, the situation was also amusing. In my drugged confusion, I was trying to imagine how I should react. Perhaps I should cry. Perhaps I should laugh—or fight. I doubled up my fist. Then I saw that Red Dog's mouth had a peculiar shape that I had never noticed before. And his teeth were bigger and sharper than they had been.

Now the room, the strange redness, had turned into a kind of translucent purple. Jake said something, and Ben answered him. The voices were becoming garbled and queer-sounding.

"Sit her in a chair, Drum," Red Dog said. "She's spacing out. Get a wet rag and wash her face. Maybe that will revive her."

Drum led me to a chair, and I sat down. Ben, Drum, Red Dog, Jake, the room—everything seemed alien. The candlelight held strange patterns and filled up the space of the room with a fabulous liquid gold. Drum returned with a cold wet rag and wiped it over my face and forehead. I fought the rag and heard Drum's derisive laughter. He was making jokes about my disordered state.

Red Dog was talking to Jake, and their words were bellowing into my ear. "I want to see him," Red Dog said.

"I have bred a horse such as the world has never seen before, a horse that can run three days without food or water."

I noticed that Ben was bent over and looking at me. His image was swimming. His eyes held a murderous light. "Fool," he said.

I tried to reply, but my mouth was too dry. It felt as if it were stuffed with cotton.

Again I focused on Jake's voice. "The perfection of the horse is a matter of aesthetics. We're no better off for our computers. Man should perfect himself as I have done with my animals." He and Red Dog were bordered in a murky purple, as though I were seeing them through a kaleidoscope. Jake picked up his teacher's skull. He seemed to carry it by some kind of braided rawhide handle.

"Come, let me see your breed," Red Dog said. "Bring Lynn. She might want a last look at a horse."

Drum and Ben lifted me up from the chair, and we followed Red Dog and Jake outside. It seemed extremely dark, and I thought we were winding around in a circle. The wind on my wet face had a slightly reviving effect. We entered a covered enclosure lit by many lanterns. I started sneezing because of the dust and straw. When I looked up, I saw a form within the shadows. The form leapt straight out at me and became the body of a white stallion. This horse was enormous, much larger than any other I had ever seen. He pawed the floor and reared, snorting and challenging our presence. Jake approached him and placed the skull around the horse's neck, tying the leather handle at the withers. The skull hung like a hideous, evil flower on the elegant blue-silver stallion. Even with his strange death necklace, he was the most exquisitely lovely creature I had ever seen. I found myself crying.

"My God," I said in a slurred voice. "He's so beautiful."

Everyone was amused that I had spoken.

Jake's eyes were animated. "I created him. His name is Arion. He can see twice the distance of any horse, sense water a hundred miles away. His hearing is so acute, he can hear through twenty-foot-thick walls. His nervous system can withstand almost any impact. I know. I've tested him."

"Yes, I can see that you have," Red Dog said. "What about the powers, the powers?"

"It's not more than a generation away," Jake said. "This breed will be able to project images that will fool anyone. They will be able to disappear and reappear at will. Horses are the embodiment of the alchemist's dream. They represent our instinctual nature transformed into a godlike power."

"There's no reason you can't succeed, Jake," Red Dog said. "Look how far you've come." He patted Jake on the back by way of congratulations. "Thank you for letting me see Arion, and also for the gift you've given me, of Lynn. She is really weak and stupid, you know."

"She seems harmless enough," Jake said, throwing me a look.

"She is perfectly harmless without her teachers," Red Dog said.

Drum, holding me by the arm, said, "I never thought she had any power."

"Yeah, she was just lucky," said Ben, holding me by the other arm.

"Well, I have some unfinished work with her," Red Dog said. "Just a loving stroke on a spot on her body, and no power can save her, the coup de grâce. Hers will be an uncomplicated end."

I knew Red Dog was referring to a death point, a place on the human body known to a very few sorcerers, acupuncturists, and martial artists, a point that if manipulated would kill me. Nothing short of a miracle would be able to save me from physical death.

"Ready, Lynn?" he asked. "It's time to join your ancestors." He stepped toward me, making a hooked fist with two fingers protruding from it.

But seeing him move toward me was like a slap in the face. I shook, trying to clear away the foggy gray. The adrenaline pumped through my body. I saw the horse, Arion, turn his head and look at me, his ears pinned back just as if he had understood every word Red Dog had said. Illuminated by the mellow light from the hanging kerosene lanterns, Arion seemed to burst into rainbow colors. I assumed this vision was a hallucination. As Red Dog was reaching for my left shoulder, with Ben and Drum still holding me, Arion reared up and let out a high-pitched warning. He shot forward, and his head butted Red Dog, who flew back several feet, taking Drum with him. Ben still held tight, and the two of us whirled around in a circle. Jake grabbed a whip and wielded it after Arion, who was trying to trample Red Dog. The sorcerer managed to dodge the hooves. Ben let loose of my arm as Arion charged between us. To my surprise, the horse reared up and kicked Jake in the face. The old man fell against a hanging lantern. It smashed to the floor and immediately ignited the straw into a roaring blaze. Arion, now clearly my protector, came and stood near me. I grabbed a handful of silky mane and leapt up on his back as I had done as a child on my horse, Sugar, whom I had ridden bareback and free over the ranch land near Seattle.

The scene was now one of total pandemonium. Jake's face was bleeding, and he beat at the flames with his shirt. Ben and Drum were running in circles, using gunnysacks on the flames to no avail. Red Dog picked up a pitchfork and held it like a spear. Arion and I raced around the enclosure. It was filled with pink, sooty smoke that boiled up into the night sky. I clung to Arion's neck for dear life, choking and coughing, tears streaming down my face. I heard yelling and coughing from the others. The whole compound had caught fire. A gas tank exploded, and I caught a glimpse of the house beginning to burn. There was nothing but smoke, smoke everywhere. I was losing consciousness from lack of oxygen.

Arion reared and crashed through the enclosure. We galloped out into the labyrinthian horse maze. In all directions horses were wild-eyed and screaming. We plunged down the corridors of the maze, and I opened gate after gate, the latches pulling easily from the top. I saw Doris, Axel, and other men opening stall doors in the barns. There was no sign of Red Dog or Jake. Ben and Drum were not to be seen either. Perhaps they had burned to death, I thought.

I found a strength I did not know I had as I clung to Arion. We were heading for the main wall at incredible speed. With horror I realized we were going to jump. Arion coiled like a giant snake underneath me, and we catapulted into the darkness. His mane still had burning sparks in it, and I could smell the charred places on my clothes. Arion landed with great power, with the surefootedness of a wonder horse. We galloped off in the direction of the mountains.

I wrapped my wrists and hands in the braided leather supporting the jeweled skull tied around Arion's neck. It held me well. The effects of the drug were coming on again, in heavier waves now. I was not able to focus my eyes on any point. I lay down against Arion's neck.

I had ridden all my life, but never on a horse such as this. He seemed to know where he was going, so I trusted him. His pounding hooves echoed through the forest as we fled. I do not know how I managed to stay on Arion, but I did.

We headed down a sheer mountain face of shale. When I looked behind me, I saw the ominous conflagration, cracking loudly. A redness stretched along the spine of the mountain. Tiny flecks of light like fireflies flew from Arion's hooves as they struck the shale stone. I wasn't sure what was happening. I was moving as if in a dream. There was a coldness on my face, and I felt as though I could peel layer after layer of my own face away. Then my head filled with a low vibrating tone that was intensely painful to my ears. The effect was to distort my vision so that sky and earth became a two-dimensional plane, opening and closing in front of me. This broke up into a series of oscillating holes, and I knew I would have to select one of them to go through. I urged Arion toward the hole with the most luminosity. He veered to the left, and we broke through. The light seemed to be compressed and had a peculiar thickness. We were riding through a long cylindrical cavern. In the distance I saw a lake, shimmering black and purple in the moonlight. Vaporous bubbles cut the surface.

Arion increased his speed and headed straight for the pool. Collecting his powerful haunches, head and neck arched like a swan, we dove forcefully into the water. Everything went dark. Looking back, I don't know where reality ended and the sacred dream began. What I remember becomes very hazy in places.

As we went down into the depths of the lake, curious fish gathered around us. It seemed as if we could breathe there. There was no problem, as if all life force were the same in this translation. It did not matter if we were horse, human, or fish. We shared the same source of animation. The water was like the wind and felt pleasing against my cheeks and legs. Arion's mane fanned back, as did my own hair. My grasp on Arion slipped. I had to clutch at his fine hair. The tuft I held felt like billowing silk. We surged forward and downward with an undulating rhythm. Great spiral shells of mother-of-pearl as large as caves surrounded us at the bottom, and then what looked like coral reefs shimmered in and out of view. The water had gone through various gradations of color but became darker as we descended deeper.

Arion galloped along the sandy bottom, and I turned my head away from what I saw next. It was a wretched sight. Arion stopped, pawing at the sand and underwater moss. In front of me were acres of human bones piled several feet high. There were piles of skulls and hip bones and rib bones. I looked to my right into the murky depths and saw a woman fashioning her own body out of the vertebrae and bone parts that were scattered about her, sticking out of the sand at odd angles. She peered back at me through the gloom with cavernous eye sockets. She stood and reached out through the pale curtain of gray water, clutching at me with bony, grasping fingers.

She said, "These are the bones of dead shamans who have fallen and drowned and have not made it through their shaman death."

"Who are you?" I asked.

"I am the goddess of your own fear. I am small, tiny. I am all these bones and all that you refuse to see. I am that which you have hidden from yourself. I am your love of fear. Let me ride with you on your white stallion, and I will be transformed forever."

I gave her my arm and swung her up behind me. Arion turned back toward the great shells we had seen, and we swam over to them. I felt as if I were riding on the back of a giant sea serpent, Arion knew the water so well. He swam effortlessly into a huge conch shell. I touched the hard pearly walls. The surface felt satiny, like I imagined the underbelly of a whale would feel. The light became suddenly bright and more intense, and I felt heat. The brightness dimmed and two beautiful women appeared. One was young and one was old. The young one was encased in fire.

She reached out to me and said, "I am the goddess of your death. You are a young shaman. But if others find me in you, they can use the knowledge against you. That will be your tragedy. Take me on your white stallion, and I will be transformed forever."

I stretched out my arm, and she leapt up behind me.

Arion swam over to the other woman, who now floated above a bed of seaweed. She appeared to be sleeping on her side. She was very old.

"Excuse me," I said.

She opened her eyes.

"I don't mean to bother you, but would you mind telling me who you are?"

She smiled. "I am the goddess of your undirected thoughts, and that could mean your death at any moment. You must stay hidden. Protect your value. Dream only with intent. Take me with you on your white stallion, and I will be transformed forever."

I gave the old woman my arm, and she leapt up like a puff of desert wind. Arion shot up toward the surface, and we exploded out of the water. He galloped along the shore, finding sure footing on the slippery stones. We clattered around the shore toward a meadow. It seemed to me to be morning, because the light was luxurious, but the half moon was out in glowing orange. Arion stopped by a stand of tall trees with twisted roots protruding from the ground. The land there was open and ascended gradually. I noted that the ground was parched and burnt.

We all dismounted. Immediately Arion began pacing back and forth in front of us, bucking his head and whinnying for me to help him. The jeweled skull was irritating to him, and I knew what to do.

"Here, Arion," I called. I patted the earth.

Arion came over, silhouetted in shafts of yellow light. He began to paw and dig a hole with the hoof of his powerful foreleg. In only a moment it was deep enough, and I patted him and took the skull off his foaming neck. I dropped it into the hole and, on all fours, buried it with the help of my three accomplices. We all shoved dirt over it and watered the newly packed earth with our tears.

Soon a green sprout pierced up out of the earth, and a beautiful tree grew up toward the light. Multicolored fruit hung from its branches.

In front of the tree, another maiden appeared.

"Who are you?" I asked.

"I am the goddess of your manipulations and tricks, of your effort in the world. There is no need now for striving. You are alone. You have yourself now. Do not be afraid. Eat with me from this tree of knowledge and be transformed forever."

"I will eat," I said.

First I fed Arion. The fruit were shaped like apples, but had a shiny, deep blue color. Then each of us ate of the fruit.

The next thing I knew, I was lying on some old wool blankets by a briskly burning campfire. My whole body ached. For a moment I could not remember who I was. The moon came out from behind a cloud, and I saw a human form, crimson and ghostlike in the fire's glow. Twin Dreamers sat across the campfire from me. I flinched at the sight of her, waking up quickly. I had a terrible headache. Perhaps it was a hangover from the drug Jake had given me. I was clumsy and did not have my customary coordination.

Twin Dreamers came around to me and knelt by my side. She carefully pushed me back to a supine position and placed a piece of quillwork on my chest. How she had been doing quillwork by firelight, I have no idea. I noticed that the porcupine quills were securely sewn onto the leather, making a beautiful star-burst pattern. The quills felt slick and round to my fingers.

"It is good that you rest," she said.

I relaxed into her care. Her face was almost hidden by shadows. She seemed to possess the night. Yet she looked like a madwoman, her sunken eyes ablaze with an inner flame. Hanging in straggles to her waist, her hair was just as wild and unkempt as it had been the first time I saw her. Her body was considerably crooked and painfully thin. She wore a long, faded blue skirt and an old plaid shirt with holes at the elbows. She pulled a fringed shawl about her shoulders and observed me, pursing her old, lined lips. She must have caught my awe-inspired expression because the corners of her mouth started to turn up. Her eyes squinted with a twinkle behind them. Her shoulders started to jiggle up and down, and pretty soon we were both laughing out loud. Tears were running down our faces. Because she laughed, I could not stop laughing. I don't know what hit me, the absurdity of the situation, of life and death, of this extraordinary shaman looking like a bag woman, of the situations I repeatedly found myself in. I don't know, but we laughed and laughed. Within that process a great kinship was born between us. Our ringing laughter was the bond.

A long silence followed, and my mind raced over the visions and events of the past night.

"I am a double woman dreamer," said Twin Dreamers, finally breaking the silence with her heavily accented, guttural voice. "If you are a woman who dreams in this way, everyone thinks you are crazy." She gave me a silly smile with brilliant eyes. "You think I'm crazy too."

"One thing I know for sure," I said. "We're both crazy."

Twin Dreamers slapped my leg and laughed convulsively.

"*Lila witkowin*," she said between laughs. "Crazy woman."

I started to laugh again, then saw that Twin Dreamers had become serious. I sobered immediately.

"People are afraid of me," she said. "Especially men. They say I possess men. That is not true. Men don't like my face, and I say, 'But what can I do? It is just my face.'" She shrugged, slapped my leg, and we laughed again.

She leaned toward me and snatched the quillwork off my chest and began working it again. The beads and quills shone like tiny star fragments in her hands.

"I can work like a man. I have a lot of strength. My quillwork is the very best." She pulled a thread and knotted it, breaking the thread with her teeth. "Here, this is for you. It's a pouch for your horse medicine."

"My horse medicine?"

"Yes, for a piece of Arion's hair. Horses are *wakan*, sacred. They have the spirit. *Xunkaukan yuwakanpi kin.*"

"You know Arion? How do you know?"

"You saw a living rainbow on your horse's belly."

"Yes." I stared at her. The skin between my shoulder blades was beginning to crawl.

"I am that. I am shape-shifter Twin Dreamers."

"I don't understand." I remembered when the surface of Shahzonn's body had broken out in an eruption of colored lights. My mind felt as if it were going to split wide open, as it always felt when my shamanistic labors took me into the unknown and uncharted areas that lie just out of reach of normal, rational consciousness.

Twin Dreamers laughed. "I am that," she said, still laughing.

Grateful, I heard a low whinny and turned my head. I saw the shadow of Arion where he grazed on the rich grass of the nearby slopes.

"I was smoking you, trying to keep you away from Ben and Drum. I knew Red Dog's purpose in sending them. Red Dog and Hawks-Above were going to take your light. I have been near you for a while. I borrowed your horse's spirit so I could help you on your path. Your way has need of my teaching. You need protection."

"I don't know what kind of woman you are, but here." I reached into my pocket, where I always carry a rope of sweetgrass, and put it in her hand. "With heartfelt gratitude," I said.

Twin Dreamers lit the end of it in the campfire.

"I've always liked sweetgrass," she said. "It is *wakan*." She laughed and then smudged us, blowing smoke over us both in blessing.

"You saved me," I said.

"I have no destiny of my own. I take on the shape of another, and for moments I live that life. I am alone. I will always be alone. That is my burden and my freedom. I have no life of my own. I doctor your spirit and then I go on my way. I have no death, but I saw yours in a dream, and she rode with us and became transformed. It is good. It is *wakan*."

I sat upright and stared at her, trying to absorb the implications of the words she was saying.

"You live in the faraway and then you come back? Is that it?"

"Yes, I come back. But when you come back, you will not remember this round."

"Can you teach me?"

"Maybe I can teach you something. Maybe not. I know the constellations. You are not yet a shape-shifter, but I can teach you to remember your body. Yes, you can learn to go to the next circle of life experience with your body and then bring it back to this round at will."

"Why would I want to do that?"

"Because then you can choose your death."

I stared at her.

"Tell me of your shaman journey," she said.

"Where shall I begin?"

"Begin where you entered the lower world and entered the shaman lake."

She placed the flat of both her hands on the earth and rocked her body back and forth. She closed her eyes, listening.

I told her every aspect of the events as I remembered them, every feeling, every manifestation of the vision.

Slowly Twin Dreamers began to speak about the bones of fallen shamans. "Those shamans fell because they would not be stripped of their flesh. Spirit lives in the bones. They could not allow themselves to go as bare bones into another realm, stripped of their identity. Those shamans were made of fears and attachments. Your goddess built herself out of fear—the fear that you have secretly hidden even from yourself, because you love it. You need it to feel alive. She was of the element of water.

"Your next goddess was from the element of fire. She knew of your endurance and that death can be seen in you if you lack endurance within the movement between life situations. Perseverance in following your life's dream is a special kind of endurance. First you must identify your dream. If you fear death, it means that you are not yet living. This is not a matter of will.

"The old goddess was of the element of air. She appeared because you have spent a lifetime daydreaming and wallowing in your sorrows. You have no more time for this loss of vitality. That is over for you forever.

"The last maiden was born from the element of earth and from the evil skull you planted there. She grew from the tears of your own *heava*, your own darkness. The thirsty earth took your tears, and the evil was transformed by Mother Earth. The goddess of earth knew of your tricks and your profound efforts. But you have to learn to be loose, to be unencumbered by what you know. The knowledge that is important is First Knowledge. And First Knowledge is understanding that each and every act may be your last.

"In my language the horse is called 'medicine dog.' Riding on a medicine dog is balancing. You could never come to proper balance without accepting the separated aspects of your being. And that means accepting the *heava*, the profound darkness of your own spirit.

"Some of us, the two-leggeds," she went on, now sifting the sandy earth through her fingers, "are capable of murder, and not simply in self-defense. We can be bought by the many-colored monsters for cheap wages. Yet we judge others and become attached to them. Our nature has looked away from itself, and there is no way to make amends or track down your freedom again."

The moon was lowering in the night sky behind her.

At length she spoke again. "There is an old legend told by the twisted-hair, the storytellers. It has been told many times and in many different ways. I will tell it to you in my way. Perhaps it will help you understand your *heava*, the mountain of darkness we sit upon and call our consciousness.

"A long time ago, up in the north country, there was a mountain lion, and she was about to give birth to a cub. It was in the Moon of the Buffalo Cow's Fetus Getting Large. She knew she had to have food for her ordeal, so she went out and found a herd of sheep. She killed one of the sheep, but in the process of doing so, she died herself. The baby cub was born anyway. He was taken on by the sheep herd as one of their own. This mountain lion grew up thinking he was a sheep.

"A few years went by, and one day an old grandfather mountain lion came down out of the forest and saw this young mountain lion grazing on the grass like a sheep. The grandfather could not believe it. He walked down into the meadow and went up to him. Sure enough, he smelled just like a sheep. That was disgusting to the grandfather, so he grabbed the young lion by the scruff of the neck and dragged him over to the river. The grandfather forced him to look at his own reflection. He showed him he looked just like him, a mountain lion. He was not a sheep. This was a hard realization, that he had spent his whole life in a masquerade. Then the grandfather and the younger mountain lion went off into the forest, and the grandfather lion taught him how to hunt. He regained his original nature.

"This is a medicine story that holds up a mirror for you to look upon. We were all born wild like a mountain lion, and to live in civilization we become sheep at a very young age. How could it be otherwise, or everyone would look like me." Twin Dreamers held out the ends of her tangled hair, which held pieces of grass. She looked like a wild thing. We grinned at each other and then laughed.

"Do you understand, Lynn?"

"I think so. You're saying that our instinctual nature is represented by the mountain lion, and that it is in essence hidden and shoved down inside ourselves by the time we can talk."

"Yes, because our instinct is denied, it becomes deformed. It is expressed in life as your *heava*."

"So, what our psychologists call neurosis . . ."

Twin Dreamers' mouth had dropped open, and she was pinning me with a quizzical look.

"I'm sorry," I said. "Our doctors call this a demonic or dark side of the self. But now I see it is really just our innate wildness suppressed."

"Yes, we become tame. But we are not house pets. We are fierce and wild by nature. Movement between one life situation and another is essential. Movement or action is the key that unlocks the door to understanding. But I have said enough for now. Dream on this: Consider what is left of your instinctual nature. Remember that action is not a reaction. It has a lodge of its own." She pointed. "That beautiful horse grazing out there is a symbol of instinctual action. That is why when you see a horse, you become both happy and sad. That horse represents the wildness within yourself that you have never dared to become."

Our eyes met, and with a little start I felt a sense of her great strength. I felt my cheeks glowing and my heart beating. I was on the verge of tears. Twin Dreamers had made me feel a sense of my whole character and not simply my vanity or my social self. She was right. I thought about all the men I had known who had misunderstood my love of horses. Then I thought of how many young girls love horses with a passion. Perhaps because of the structure of our society, we women have been able to stay closer to our instinctual nature than most men. I mentioned this to Twin Dreamers.

She said, "True. As teachers, as medicine women, we have to reacquaint both men and women with their total nature. We must help the males of the world to return to a creative use of instinct, instead of expressing themselves through destruction and war."

I started to ask more questions, but Twin Dreamers motioned with her hand. "No more talk. Sleep."

She turned from me and rolled herself up in blankets. I dared not speak or bother her. She was asleep almost instantly. I sat still for a long time. My mind was racing, and I was totally awake, although extremely tired.

I got up and walked a little way out into the meadow. Arion glowed silver and violet in the moonlight. He nickered softly as I put my arms around his neck. He turned his great head and nibbled at my jeans. I petted him and scratched his withers, which made him shiver with delight. Then I turned back toward the glowing campfire. I heard a *click-clump* behind me. Arion, head lowered, was following me. I scratched his forehead. He followed me right up to the campfire and did not want to leave.

I was suddenly overcome with exhaustion. "Arion, my wonderful medicine dog. I simply have to get some rest now."

A breeze ruffled the trees. I got under my blankets. With a groan Arion lay down beside me with amazing ease, as if he had always done so. For a horse to stay lying down in your presence, let alone to lie down next to you, is an incredible display of trust. I petted him and ended up laying my head on his neck like the ancient Celts and Bedouins have done for centuries. I went to sleep like a baby.

4

Melting

The next morning I heard voices but could not bring myself to wake up. There was much laughter. I opened my eyes and it was early dawn, an apron of golden light appearing in the east. Arion was grazing out in the open meadow. A pot of coffee bubbled, and eggs and fried bread sizzled in a cast iron skillet over the fire. My stomach growled. I was starving. Twin Dreamers hastened to tend the fire, moving the skillet back from the coals. She laughed at someone behind me. I rolled over.

I suppose I should have been ready for practically anything, but it was still a shock to see Agnes, Ruby, and July sitting there. They were grinning like three idiots. I leapt up, and the four of us all hugged at once. I stammered that I was happy to see them. They were all laughing and talking at once.

"How did you get here?" I asked.

"Do you think we flew here on brooms?" Ruby asked. "July drove us in the pickup truck she just bought."

"I just figured you'd lose your plane ticket to Canada," Agnes said.

Ruby said, "When you hang out with bad company almost anything can happen. By the way, is this your bag? July says it has your name on it. I can't read it." Ruby grinned. Her jokes about her blindness always amused her.

I was still always amazed at how Ruby seemed to see better than any of us. I took my flight bag timidly. "Where did you get it? It has all my important papers in it, credit cards, everything."

"Then, you certainly shouldn't leave it in the middle of a field, should you? How very careless."

"Agnes, you don't have any idea what's happened to me. I saw Ben and Drum in California and they—"

"I imagine I have some idea," Agnes said, cutting me off. "You've been a fool again."

"Yes, you really should avoid Ben and Drum in the future," Ruby said. "They mean you no good."

"Well, it's a good thing Twin Dreamers was looking out for you. Otherwise, the sisterhood would have been minus its newest member," Agnes said. "I'm starving. Let's eat."

I looked inside my flight bag. I was relieved to see that everything seemed to be there, particularly my wallet. We sat on the blankets and ate breakfast. Arion came over and nosed around suspiciously.

Soon after breakfast Twin Dreamers picked up her shawl and placed it around my shoulders. She helped clean up the dishes, then hugged July, Ruby, and Agnes, and turned to me.

"Unhappily, I must go."

"Thank you for your guidance," I said.

"It's cut now, but we will meet again."

"But, Twin Dreamers, there's so much I want to ask you. Please . . ."

"No, my child. Your journey is to the north now. Come. We will speak with Arion."

I followed her into the meadow. As we approached, Arion's head swung up, his dished face reaching up toward the sun. His nostrils flared, testing the currents of air. His eyes were alert, catching the sharpness of light and shadow. Twin Dreamers stared at me for a long moment. Then she placed her hands on Arion's neck and stroked him gently. His tail started to switch in harmony with his bobbing head.

Suddenly, wildly, he reared and began turning in the directions of the wind. The willingness of his spirit shone through his eyes, his willingness to be made of the wildness of things. He galloped away from us.

What my eyes perceived became unclear. Twin Dreamers moved away from me diagonally in the direction of Arion. I was propelled backward by some force. I did not see Twin Dreamers' feet and legs move. For an instant I wondered if she were shrinking, as though I were now seeing her through the reverse end of a telescope. The meadow was distorting, too, stretching out to an inclined plane with everything collapsing in on itself. I felt cold. I saw a flare of light that oscillated faster and faster. The light seemed to surround Arion. It hurt my eyes. The meadow grass blazed like emeralds, and the ground itself was melted sapphire. Arion was tarnished gold, copper, silver.

I was on my knees, holding my stomach and gasping for breath. The last I saw of Arion, he was galloping over a ridge, tail held high like a scythe of fire in the wind. I became conscious that Agnes and Ruby were standing at my sides, pulling me up by the arms.

"What happened?" I asked.

"Why, I honestly don't know," Ruby said, batting her opalescent eyes. "That was some sight, though."

"Whatever could have happened to Twin Dreamers?" Agnes said. "Maybe she fell in a hole. Shall we go look, Ruby?"

"We should. But we have Lynn to look after, remember? She might fall into the same hole."

"Whenever I see Lynn, the craziest things start to happen. It's a good thing we don't see her all the time," Agnes said.

"Agnes," I said, still breathing heavily. "That's not true. It's not my fault."

"Yes, it is," Ruby said. "Get around you and everything just turns upside down. Oh, you look simple enough, but I swear confusion and chaos follow you around everywhere you go."

"What's wrong, Lynn?" July asked. She had walked up unnoticed. "You look like you've seen a ghost."

"Something like that," I stammered.

After much jesting and joking, Ruby and Agnes finally succeeded in returning me to a normal state. We were soon bouncing down a pitted dirt road in the old green pickup truck July had bought. We were all four squeezed in the front and only seat. It was a big, mean truck, the underside of which had been rotted out by snow and salt. The snow tires were huge and, once we reached the highway, sang with a drumming cadence. Each tire was different from the others and there were no hubcaps. Both outside rearview mirrors hung uselessly and went *clickety-clackety* in the wind. The driver's door was wired shut with bailing wire. There was every kind of gash and hole in the side panels. Our seat was split open to reveal the foam cushions and cotton stuffing. An old army blanket was spread over most of the holes. Part of the floorboards were open to the road. An old wild turkey feather hung from the rearview mirror, attached to a beaded shield with a carved pipestone hanging from it. The windows were so dirty and greasy, I could hardly see through them, but I enjoyed watching the play of sunlight as it turned into prisms through the swipes of oil on the windshield.

Mile after mile passed. After a while I said, "Agnes, I have to talk about Twin Dreamers."

"Go ahead. Talk."

"Well, Twin Dreamers told me she is a shape-shifter and knows no death. Back there, when I got sick, did she just become Arion, or what happened?"

"Twin Dreamers is of the old sisterhood."

"But you said the sisterhood was thousands of years old."

"That's true. No telling how long she has been wandering over the earth."

"But is the sisterhood thousands of years old?" I stammered.

"That's right," Ruby said. "We weren't born yesterday, you know."

July was wide-eyed, as was I. I thought the truck was going to skid off the road. We hit a rut and all four of our heads hit the tin roof liner simultaneously. Ruby and Agnes were full of boundless mirth, elbowing each other. Again I was at a loss for words. For some reason I thought of Gertrude Stein on her deathbed. Someone asked her if she had found the answer to her questions. "More importantly, what is the question?" she had replied. My bewilderment was acute. How could I ask Agnes anything when her implication shattered all my rational concepts?

Agnes traced a spiral in the dust of the dashboard with her finger. She pointed to it. "Lynn, to understand Twin Dreamers and how she lives, you must return to this." She traced the lines of her dust drawing again. It had the effect of making me dizzy. "Here is your death," she said.

"That doesn't feel like death dust to me," Ruby said, taking a pinch of the fine powder between her fingers. "Death dust has more grit."

Agnes continued. "As you know, we Native Peoples who follow the old ways consider the spiral to be sacred. It is more than a simple construct of space and time. It has the answer within it, Lynn."

"The answer you are looking for," Ruby quickly added.

July swerved the truck, dodging a turtle on the road.

"July, slow down," Ruby snapped. "Never have I seen a worse driver. I want to get back to the reserve in one piece, don't you, Agnes?"

"I certainly do," Agnes said. "Now, to continue with you, Lynn. It is a good thing to learn the lessons of the spiral, so I will repeat myself again and again until you learn."

"Yes, yes, Lynn. Learn your lessons. Your lessons make my little ears hurt. So, hurry up, Agnes," Ruby said in anguish.

Agnes pushed her finger in the middle of the dust spiral. "When you are born, you come from the void. You come from the mystery. You are born out of formlessness from the center of the spiral. You dress yourself with the fine feathers of time and space, and you take on a mind. You think you are mind. Your earth walk is a spiraling outward from this center. As you progress," she said, circling her finger to the outermost edge, "you become more and more earthbound. You take on form through experience and conditioning from your environment. You become encrusted with addictions and what you call time."

"That's the household name for it, all right," Ruby piped in again. "Time. Daytime, nighttime. Any old time."

"To stay in form," Agnes said, her voice slightly lower, "you must develop a mind that is your ego, which again is a function of time."

"Get to the point," Ruby said. "Agnes is trying to tell you that Twin Dreamers has lost her mind."

"I don't understand," I said.

Ruby said, "Of course, you don't understand. If you understood, you'd be teaching us, and we'd have a fool for a teacher." She laughed at her own statement.

"Twin Dreamers is no longer a part of the dream lodge of time," Agnes said. "There is a trinity of symbols confronting our earthwalk here. In front of us is an eagle, a clock, and a mole. Twin Dreamers was one of the few who was able to demolish the clock."

Ruby laughed. "Yeah, Twin Dreamers smashed the clock. She is a woman who has smashed time. I never thought about it that way, Agnes."

"I still don't understand. How can she smash the clock, time?" I asked.

"By dissolving her ego, so she can take on the shape of other egos. She has perfected this art to such a degree, she can shift her physical shape and become part of another dreamer's dream." Agnes stared at me with a cold eye and said, "How do you know that you're not a shape-shifter in one form or another? Maybe you simply don't remember what you are dreaming!"

Ruby elbowed me in the ribs. "The secret is that all of us are shape-shifters, but some of us know it and some of us don't." She reached over and, with a swipe, erased the spiral. "That's kind of what she did," she said, meaning Twin Dreamers.

We had crossed the border into Canada and cut back west. We camped out the first night in an open field. We baked potatoes in aluminum foil. July and I slept in the bed of her pickup. We talked and laughed into the night, looking at the stars, the path of souls. There were a lot of insects, and the buzzing kept me up half the night, but I finally got to sleep.

The next morning we were up at dawn and rolling. About noon we stopped for lunch at a small roadside café called Maria's. It was dim and gloomy inside. July, Ruby, Agnes, and I sat down at a rickety, rectangular table with a pitted metal base. It reminded me of the tables I sat at as a teenager in the Seattle Rollerdome. Agnes stuck her toothpick into the holes of the faded red-and-white-checkered plastic tablecloth. Music of a fifties vintage bleated from the jukebox in the deserted dining room. Next to us was a greasy glass display case containing sunglasses, cassette tapes, and a Mother's Day special of gold rings and cheap watches.

A heavyset woman wearing a blue bandanna around her head and a dirty apron around her waist came over and plopped down four menus. "Special today is homemade chicken and dumplings," she said.

We all four looked at each other and in unison said, "I'll have that."

She jotted down our orders, and one by one we went to the bathroom to clean off the dirt from traveling. Before Agnes returned, she went into the kitchen. We heard her talking to the cook. She came out with a large, clear glass of water with ice cubes in it. She sat down, her hair freshly combed and her brown eyes twinkling. She put the glass in the middle of the table, next to the salt, pepper, and a half-empty bottle of catsup. She smiled and looked around at each of our faces.

"Well, Agnes," Ruby said, "I suppose you're going to ruin my meal with some Indian wisdom."

Agnes chuckled softly. "Lynn, take a good look at this glass."

"That glass?" I said, nodding my head toward it.

"Yes, this glass." She held it up in front of me with her brown, gnarled fingers. Her thick fingernails were perfectly filed. "Describe it to me."

"Well, it is a clear glass of water with ice cubes in it." I wondered what she was driving at.

"Suppose this glass of water is you and the life you are living."

"How do you mean, Agnes?"

"You are like an ice cube floating on the water."

"You're right, Agnes," Ruby retorted. "I know exactly what you mean. Lynn has always been very cold to me."

"Ruby, I am not. Sometimes I'm a little afraid of you, that's all."

"Now, listen, Lynn," Agnes continued. "Imagine you're the ice cube in the glass now. Let's say the water in this glass represents the all-surrounding ocean of enlightenment. And you're floating on it like an ice cube."

"Let me see that glass," Ruby demanded. She snatched it away from Agnes and held it very close to her opaque blue eyes. The ice cubes clinked as she cocked her head to the side. "That's Lynn, all right. I'd recognize her anywhere."

Agnes grabbed the glass back. "As an ice cube, you look down at the primeval sea and you know a great truth."

"What's that?" I asked.

"You know that you are made out of the same substance. You are made out of water. There is only one difference. Do you know what that is?"

"I am frozen."

"Correct. The only difference is temperature."

"That's nothing new," Ruby interrupted once again. "We've always known Lynn is an iceberg."

"Ruby!" I scowled at her.

July giggled, observing the situation.

"It's important to know what you are doing, living on this good mama," Agnes said. She bent and placed her hand on the floor. "And why did you find a medicine woman to teach you?"

"To learn."

"But why do we bother to learn anything? And, more importantly, why do we struggle with our addictions? That is the same question posed to you by our sister Zoila after your experiences in La Caldera a few years ago. What is the answer?"

"For knowledge."

"Yes, but why knowledge, when what we finally have to do is unlearn it all?"

"To become teachers and healers."

"But why, Lynn?"

"To bring the balance of male and female back on this earth."

"Yes, but why?"

"To help people."

"You can never help people."

"Then why am I going through all this?"

We paused as a couple came in from the other room, paid their lunch tab, and left the café.

"We come into this earthwalk for only one reason. This Turtle Island is a great schoolhouse. We have chosen to come here only to become one with the Great Spirit. In your words, to become enlightened. Yet it's the one thing we're most afraid of. You come here like everyone else." Agnes was now aiming her words at Ruby. "Like an ice cube trying to melt into the all-surrounding ocean of enlightenment. But how do you do that?"

"I'm sure you have a simple answer," Ruby replied, picking her teeth with a mint toothpick.

"You come to a teacher," Agnes said. "And that teacher holds up a mirror. And if you're willing to look into it, the mirror becomes like the sun, and you begin to heat up. You begin to melt into that ocean."

"Melt? How?"

Ruby snorted, "Good question."

"Yes, it is." Agnes agreed. "Do you recall all the work you did with Zoila and Jaguar Woman?"

"Yes, I remember very well. How could I forget?"

"Much of that work, particularly La Caldera, was to help you identify your stance. A warrioress faces the world lightly, like a plume. But you discovered you were rooted in a swamp of addictions."

"I understand. But how does that melt me?"

"When you are not a warrioress, when you do not face the world lightly, there are many pitfalls, the pitfalls of addictions. When you fall into one of your addictions, let's say sadness, what you are really doing is bleeding off your precious life force. And that ice cube that you are just becomes colder. In this process of staying cold, and feeling not a sense of oneness but a state of being in duality, you are separate from the sea of the Great Spirit. There is no opening of the great mirror. There is no transcendence."

"I think I see."

"The warrioress must face herself in the great mirror to heat up, to melt."

The waitress approached with all four plates precariously balanced along her arm. She placed them in front of each of us, clunking the plates loudly on the table. She turned and left to get our drinks. I found myself staring at the ice cubes in the glass like someone in a daze.

"Think about it," Agnes said.

"Yes, Lynn." Ruby stabbed a dumpling with her fork. "Please think about it."

Something about the metaphor and the way Agnes explained it to me made me feel odd. For a moment I felt as though my physical body were vanishing and my mind were filled with a blaze of light. Then I caught myself. The experience so terrified me that I gasped loudly for a breath.

Ruby was shaking her head. "Almost, Agnes. Not quite. She always clutches for herself."

Agnes responded kindly. "Lynn, you'd better eat. You haven't touched your plate."

No one looked up, and we all ate lunch like a bunch of hungry lumberjacks. Except for me. I pushed my food around on the plate. We all ordered coffee, and Ruby insisted on pie à la mode. July talked about her pickup truck. It was the first thing of consequence that she had ever owned. She loved it. She made me think of a friend in California who was completely unhappy with her new Porsche and ungrateful because she didn't get the most expensive model. "Oh, I love my truck," July said. Her smile evidenced her satisfaction.

Ruby smoked a cigarette. The fifties music still blared from the jukebox in the other room. Agnes started tapping her booted toe to the beat. Then, slowly, as she would often do, she unfurled her fingers in the demonstration of some obscure symbol. She grinned at me, showing a neat row of white teeth. Her shoulders began to rock back and forth. Tapping with her fingers, she began to sing with the music, "A-la-la-la-la-la bamba . . ."

5

Changing the Direction
of the Wind

"Yes," Agnes said. "Even though our *heava*, our dark side, is our wild-ness unexpressed, it is also the cause of our inability to let go of our egos. You have to learn to walk out of your self-lodge and never look back. The self-lodge of the ego is not where you live. Your movement on the path between the self-lodge and your dream lodge is the way to your understanding of who you are. Power is in the action, the transit, the movement between the many lodges of your own private village."

Agnes was drawing several concentric circles with a twig in the earth, answering a question posed to her by July. The four of us were sitting on top of a granite ridge high in the mountains. Like a maraud-ing band of outlaws, we gazed down on a sleepy settlement of wooden houses along the ribbon of blacktop that we had been traveling on for hours. I had found a comfortable concave rock and sat down, spooning my backside into the warmth it still held from the sun. I tilted my face into a warm southerly wind.

"I'm so tired," July said. "First I drive my truck for three hundred miles. Then everyone insists we hike up this mountain. I have to get some rest, or Ruby is going to have to drive."

"Well, then, get some rest," Ruby said sharply.

July pulled her shawl around her shoulders, curled up on the flat rock outcropping, and went to sleep. Agnes and Ruby stared first at her and then at me.

"What?" I asked quizzically, blinking my eyes from the turbulent wind. I was tearing from dust particles.

Agnes's demeanor had distinctly changed. Her face was turning dark and rutted in the evening light. The sun in the west was huge and golden. Splashes of orange spread across the turquoise sky behind Agnes as she squared her shoulders. She stroked her chin and cocked her head, reminding me of some prehistoric bird of prey. Slowly her hands moved toward me, and she placed them on both of my cheeks.

She whispered, "See me."

She seemed to be reflected through time. The wind subsided, and my eyes stopped tearing. She kept staring into my eyes. A hollow silence surrounded us. There was not a breath of air. The windstorm that had been buffeting us for hours had totally subsided.

"There is a black-tailed deer in your moon lodge," Ruby said from behind me. "When she wiggles her ears, the wind blows. This medicine is within you. Don't you know that it all comes from you?" Something about Ruby's voice and the intent within it gave me goose bumps.

I kept my eyes focused on Agnes.

"You can learn to change the direction of the wind."

"How can anyone do that?"

"You do it all the time. You are unaware of it."

"When?"

"When you let go of sadness."

"But what can my sadness have to do with the wind?"

"All emotions have a kinship with the wind. You must let these emotions go through you and travel on their way. Otherwise, you magnetize bad energy, which is what you do by clutching your unresolved sadness."

"I know I have a deep sadness, but I don't even know why."

"You carry your father's death deep in your bones. You keep it in your bones so you won't have to see it."

"That's true, I guess."

"Now I will move away from you, and you will go into your thought patterns again. Now see what happens."

Agnes walked away and turned her back to me. I was able to isolate a feeling of sadness. I was aware of it, like a seepage, filling me up. Then, most bafflingly, the wind picked up in southerly gusts.

Agnes turned around to face me. "The elements exist on the earth as they are. But we play with them ruthlessly by our gains and losses of energy. Right now you are throwing energy away in an outward spiral of negative thought-flow. You are holding sorrow in your bones, and you have no regard for the effect that this is having on your sister, the wind."

"But I didn't realize that I was doing it."

"Haven't we spoken many times about energy, both personal and outside ourselves? All substance is made of it, is it not?"

"Yes."

"Don't you remember that energy is a tracker following thought?"

"Well, yes."

"There are many roads to walk, many ways, many philosophies, many religions. But the path of the warrioress, the path of the magician or medicine person, is an energy path of the heart. Women move energy out from their center. The first part of their lives is so often spent taking care of family or other people. But a woman, no matter where she is in the world, knows that she does not surrender to this outpouring of energy. She may appear defeated in this male-oriented world, but she is only gathering more power in her humble stance. There is no fiercer warrior than a woman who has learned to change the wind. For if she can change the wind, she has learned to change the direction of her own thoughts, or to still them altogether. This is a quiet, contemplative thing. The circumstances in her life lead her toward her own inward power. The alchemy of moving energy from outer to inner is the alchemy of enlightenment."

"But aren't many women receptive, and don't they have a rich inner life?"

"Yes, but aren't you now speaking of yourself?"

"Well, yes. I am."

"And can you control the direction of the wind?"

"Agnes, you know I can't."

"That is so. There is no power in daydreaming and chewing on your emotional cud like a milk cow."

"Rich inner life, indeed," Ruby chided me like the voice of my alter ego.

"How to create a whirlwind, how to whirl energy around and change it. That is your dilemma as a warrioress."

"But you can't always bring your thoughts into control," I said.

The answer that came was abrupt. "Like everything in life, what you see before you is a vast device, a tool." She made a wide swing with her arm, indicating the horizon. In the variegated light it was as though we were looking out over an ancient world. It could have been the dawn of time. Gilt thunderheads with cloudy caverns of gold and purple light vaulted above us. The wind shredded the lower strata of clouds into a thin layer as pink as a baby's blanket. Canada and northern Montana stretched out in the luxurious light for hundreds of miles.

"The world is a device?"

"Yes. Everything is a device. Religions, medicine teachings, the magnificent life form that you have been blessed with. The circumstances in your life do not present problems. They are simple challenges or devices with which you are learning to evolve."

"You have chosen those devices," Ruby said in a hoarse whisper. "Even the death of your father."

"You are not facing the correct wind road," Agnes said, taking me by the shoulders and turning me sunward a quarter turn. "Face that direction. You do not have the warrioress stance. You do not face your father's death. You turn away and are buffeted by an unfriendly wind. This wind blows your power away. In this case it is not who you are, but what direction you face—so you can see the nature of the winds that approach you. Some winds are friendly and will play with you. There are hot and cold winds. There are crazy winds that can seize your mind.

There are trickster winds that you can follow at your own peril. There are mother and father winds. There are medicine winds and virtuous winds. There are winds low to the ground, earth huggers, and those high above your head. To know the wind, you study the winged ones. They know the winds better than anybody."

The wind diminished, and finally all was still. It inexplicably frightened me, because it came with a shiny moonlit darkness.

"It's the night wind," Ruby said. "A dark wind you are facing, the wind that ripens with the big moon."

I could feel the stillness of the night enter my body with each breath. But I could not feel the moonlight. It startled me, and I shivered.

"Look at it this way, Lynn," Agnes said, sensing my fear and running her hand down my arm to calm me. "The wind is a singer, the greatest singer that ever was. There are a million tunes, symphonies. But your ears are little. I don't mean little in size. I mean little in hearing ability. If you had ears for the wind and would listen, you would never be without a song. The wind climbers, the fliers, hear this music and are called to it. The wind can be an ally wind. Try this. Close your eyes and think of your father."

I did and felt the sadness.

"Yes, sadness is like dark hands squeezing your heart. It is painful. In the face of sadness, we must mimic the sun."

I was puzzled. "How do we do that?"

Hands on my shoulders from behind, she turned me a little so that I was facing directly into the west, where the sun had gone down.

"Breathe deeply and visualize the sun in your medicine eye in your forehead. Now bring the light of the sun down into your body where your father lives. Find where your father still resides within you."

I was distracted by the vast silence. But then I was able to find the area in my body where the most poignant feelings for my father were located. His image, entirely lifelike, was clear in my mind.

"Hold the vision of your father and all that you feel for him."

My father's image was so startling that I was again gripped with fear. I didn't want to look at him. My chest ached with a strong warmth. My father definitely lived there, buried in my heart.

I whispered hoarsely to Agnes, "In my heart."

"Now take the sun in your mind's eye and follow it down into your body until it reaches your heart. Hold your father's image and follow the sun. When it reaches your heart, let it illuminate you and tell me what you see."

"I see my father's smiling face now. He is a man of about thirty-five. There is also a dark ball of something sitting between us."

"What?"

"It looks like ambergris."

"What is that?"

"It is a waxy substance that is used to prolong the scent in fine perfumes. It comes from sperm whales."

"Become the ambergris and tell me what you look like."

"I am black and round and heavier than I look. I appear solid and hard, but I am actually very soft. A nail could be pushed very easily through me with your fingers. I have a musky smell, and I am old. There are fingerprints on my surface from being handled and pressed by many hands. I won't roll easily because I am a bit sticky. I stick to things. Why does ambergris make me cry?"

I was sobbing. Big tears welled up in my eyes and slid down my face.

"Because you are changing the wind. Feel it."

A soft wind was blowing over me from the west, rustling my hair and caressing me.

"But why? How?"

"Because you are bringing all your life force toward a focal point. Now, tell me. As the ambergris, what is your function in Lynn's heart?"

After several minutes, I responded. "I am a symbol of a tender relationship that was never allowed to complete itself."

"And why not?"

"Because that relationship was like me. It was sticky and dark. A great illusion of madness surrounded it. Neither Lynn nor her father could see through it, because they were too caught up in it. But the scent of love always lingered and pervaded their lives, even though they were cheated of each other for so many years. They never had the chance to talk it out. They were separated by a dark mass of danger."

"What danger?"

"Her father was of European nobility and, with his great intellect, taught Lynn that it was all right to be special," I said. "Even so, her father also had periods of great disturbance and violence. She was in danger."

"You're still not naming your function in Lynn's heart."

"My function is to stand between Lynn and her father, to protect her and him."

"Lynn, would you be willing to get rid of this ambergris in your heart?"

"I'm afraid."

"What if you just put it outside your body on a flat rock?"

"But that ambergris is like a dear, old friend. Because of it, I can still have my dad with no danger."

"Lynn, your father is dead now. His spirit will not harm you. Do this. Try to put the ambergris aside to one corner of your heart and face your father. Just try."

I made an effort and pushed the ambergris a considerable distance away, so it was not blocking my father's image.

"Oh, God! My poor daddy." Seeing him staggered me, and I wept. "He's so sorry. I'm so sorry."

Arms outstretched, my father came to me. For the first time in memory, we embraced without fear. I cried and cried as though my very heart were breaking. Agnes held me for a long time, until the moon was higher in the night sky.

Agnes said, "Can you and your father take the ambergris and gently put it anywhere outside your body? Can you let your father go, Lynn?"

I pondered this question for a long time. I recognized my desperate hunger to sit and talk with my father. I wanted to stay with him as we were in my heart. It was the first time I had ever felt truly like a daughter. With him I had always before been that difficult archetype of mother/daughter. I always had to be careful of him, and I had to take care of him. How I had needed a normal father—and here he was. "How can I give him up?"

"Now he is truly available to you. You can always meet with him in your heart, but you must also let him go. Don't imprison his spirit in your own."

I was with my father, and I felt a merging of our spirits. He said he was happy that horses had found their way back into my life. He said that he had always had an intuition that horses were good for me in some important way. He told me not to be afraid.

It was a long time before I answered Agnes. Finally, I said, "All right, we can take the ambergris out of my heart. I'm not afraid."

"You and your father take the ambergris to the world altar and come back. When you are finished, let me know."

With great care my dad and I walked our mutual treasure up the side of a volcano where I had spent time in Guatemala. We placed the ambergris in a sacred position on one of the three stone altars. We sat with our backs against two great ceiba trees and performed a ceremony. We built "fetishes" out of our dream together. There were two, one for him and one for me. These fetishes represented our inner turmoil, anger, confusion, joy, and pain. Each figure was wrapped and fashioned from wild and tame things of the earth and all the elements. Then we blessed the "fetishes" with copal and sweetgrass and stood them as guardians next to the ambergris in honor and protection. We returned to my heart.

"Now let him go. See him fade away and know that he will return whenever you need him," Agnes told me.

I let go of my father's hand. He dimmed and then vanished. My mind went blank.

"Keep your eyes closed, Lynn," Agnes said.

Ruby and Agnes turned me around in a complete revolution several times. When we stopped, I was facing what I thought was north.

"Know the wind," Agnes said.

It was still for a moment. Then, astonishingly, the north wind came up in a cold gale, whistling and blowing wildly over me.

"That wind blows and howls because you let your father go his way, because you were brave and made medicine at a world altar."

The wind was almost savage now, pushing me backward.

"Something has certainly happened," I said.

"To change the direction of the wind, you must change the direction of your thoughts. When you send vital force always *out* in the form of thought, especially negative thought, the wind is troubled. It can even go mad, not knowing which way to proceed. Your intellect is creating its own wind, which is unrecognizable. But it is a death wind, both inner and outer. This wind knows you are dying. What you think to be the wind of self will cause you a slow death. All outward flow causes death eventually."

"Tell me what I can do to prevent this, Agnes."

There was an interval of silence. Even the wailing north wind subsided. Cold tears were on my cheeks, but I felt much, much better. The deep ache in my heart had burned away, and my tears were now of relief. Agnes on my left and Ruby on my right, holding my arms, led me to a spot several yards away.

"Lie down on this flat stone shelf. Keep your eyes closed," Agnes said. The two medicine women helped me get comfortable. "Focus inward."

Agnes began rubbing my stomach in a clockwise circle, pressing now and again with her thumb. At first it was a pleasant sensation, but then it began to burn and get uncomfortable.

"Feel the heat in your navel," Ruby said in my right ear.

"Now feel the wind change," Agnes said. "Like your own self, which is always before you. It is to the right and to the left. It is behind you, above you, and below you like the wind. There is nothing but the one self. Forever. Endless. Timeless."

Her words and the pressures on my stomach were causing me a great deal of anguish. Suddenly I felt as if my body were breaking up and I were dying.

"I'm going to explode, Agnes!"

"You are the sun. Follow the sun on the wind roads of forever. Your sun is at your navel, your inner altar. Follow the direction of the sun from east to west. Now feel the wind."

My stomach was so hot, I thought it must be glowing. It was as though someone had taken a pair of tongs and set a smoldering cinder on the flat of my belly. It was searing into me. Ruby had moved to my feet and was chanting softly. Suddenly the howling wind abated. Ruby stopped chanting. There was an eerie stillness like the padded silence of a recording studio. Then I felt a series of prickles that turned into shivers. The ground began to shake—no, it was me shaking.

Ruby and Agnes were now on both sides of me, whispering into my ears. "Fire, sun, mind. Fire, sun, mind." Over and over again.

I knew what they meant. A great golden sun was growing from my navel. Tongues of fire licked over my body. The wind suddenly started to whirl around us like a tiny tornado. My whole body was shaking as if a freight train were moving through it. The sun kept growing, expanding. Terror started to grip me.

Agnes and Ruby whispered in my ears for me to keep my attention focused. As soon as fear entered my thoughts, the sun would contract. I heard wolves howling in the distance. Parts of my body were collapsing and cracking like eggshells. The wind beat around us with such a force, I was deafened. The sun grew larger and larger. My body convulsed and I let go. There was no more choice. I couldn't stop it. The sun exploded into a white-hot nothingness.

I woke up the next morning wrapped in a Pendleton trade blanket. Agnes was giggling. "You look like a prairie dog coming out of its hole."

"I do. I must," I said, still half asleep.

Ruby, July, and Agnes gathered around me. Ruby patted me on the head.

She said, "Well, you finally did it, Lynn. You found your inside sun." She patted me again.

"See, you don't need a rocket ship," Agnes said. "All you need to do is wake up, and there you have it."

I sat up. We discussed my experiences for some time. I told them what I remembered about the myth of Icarus, who soared so high, the sun melted the wax attachments of his wings and he fell into the sea and drowned. Ruby and Agnes thought it was some kind of joke, because they laughed boisterously. I told them I had not meant it as a joke, that I had told them the story to acquaint them with a myth relating to the sun.

"He went the wrong way," Ruby said.

"Hey," July said. "I think I missed something. Did I sleep through everything again?" She laughed sheepishly.

"You missed Lynn hatching the sun," Ruby said.

"Lynn gave birth to the sun?" July said, her almond-shaped dark eyes widening. "Is that what happened?"

Agnes slapped July on the back. "Something like that," she said. She turned to me. "And now we must celebrate. You will learn how to put the sun to bed. It is good. I am pleased. You have had much fear keeping you from your inward sun. Come, we must go down the mountain soon."

I stood up and stretched. Dawn was burning crimson and pink in the east. Long picket-like shadows from the mountain peaks were cast across the plains below.

Before we left the mountain, I paid my respects to the sun and the power of the four winds. I offered cornmeal *paho* to the winds. As I did so, the west wind gusted and frolicked over the plains. She pulled on me and caressed me and made herself known to me.

Agnes walked up. "There is no doubt. Your ally wind is of the west."

Later, as we climbed down the long trail that went down the mountain, I said, "What a night."

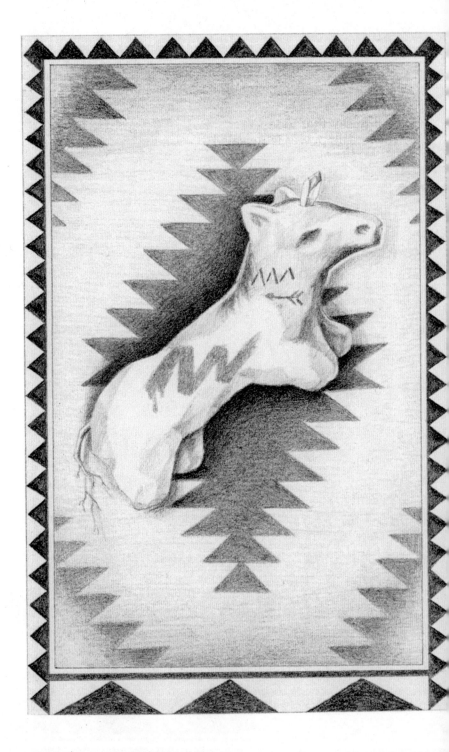

6

Lightning Root

We drove through a large city, pushing north. Agnes began giving July directions—"Turn here," "Go there," and so on.

I began to wonder if we were lost. It seemed as if we were driving aimlessly. With all four of us crowded into the front seat, we were uncomfortable. July was driving. Next to her sat Ruby, who kept kicking the gearshift and fidgeting. I was next, and Agnes was by the window. The winding road we were on led into a canyon rimmed by high yellow rocks. Agnes was tense. She kept rolling down the window and holding the broken door mirror so she could look into it and see the road behind us. I kept turning to look behind me, too, wondering what she was looking for. I saw nothing except a nondescript black pickup truck pulling off the highway and onto a dirt road.

"Agnes, you're making me nervous," I said. "What's the matter?"

She was intent on some private process of her own. She waved for me to be silent. A long blade of grass protruded from her mouth, and she kept checking the mirror.

"Agnes, close the darn window," Ruby coughed. "My neck is getting cold."

Ruby was still fidgeting. She was tracing a figure that looked like an infinity sign on her knee. She drew it again and again, never stopping. Suddenly Agnes stiffened.

"What's going on?" I asked excitedly.

"I knew it. It doesn't surprise me any." Agnes removed the chewed grass blade and threw it out the window. Then she closed it tight.

Ruby and Agnes began a lengthy conversation in Cree. July looked frightened, but I couldn't understand any of it. Ruby was shaking her head in disgust.

"Better do something quick," Ruby said.

"Pull off the road, July. Down that little road right there."

July swung the truck, nearly fishtailing in response to Agnes's urgency. She cut the engine. Tall reeds beside a running creek hid the truck.

"Come on. Get out," Agnes said as she opened the door. She took my hand and jerked me outside. She yelled to July, "Dust the tire tracks. You have very little time."

July picked up a leafy branch from the ground and ran, head ducked, to the point where we had turned off the dirt road. Walking backward, she brushed the tire tracks for several yards. She threw the branch into a clump of bushes and ran back to Agnes. The four of us made a little nest for ourselves inside the reeds. Through a slit I could see the road. The nondescript black pickup whizzed by. It looked as if three men sat in the cab.

"Would someone tell me what's going on?" I asked.

"Yes, I'll tell you," Agnes said. "That was Red Dog who just drove by in that truck."

"Red Dog." The name made me cringe. My body jerked in panic and prickles went up my back.

"Lynn," Agnes went on, not paying attention to my terror, "you have had much protection around you, sent to you from the sisterhood. Now Red Dog is doubly off-balance because he didn't know you were acquainted with horse medicine. Red Dog is really angry. He's not going to fool around anymore. His focus is usually on power. Now it's directly on you. Come, we have much to do."

I followed her along the stream. She seemed to be looking for something.

"Ruby, let me have your buck knife," Agnes said.

Ruby removed it from her boot sheath, flipped it, and handed it to Agnes by the handle.

"What are you looking for, Agnes?" I asked.

"Lightning root. And you better hope I find one. Not for my sake, but for yours."

She was crawling on all fours, smoothing out the ground with her hands. "Here," she said. She took the knife and plunged it into the earth, rotating it in a wide back-and-forth movement. "Help," she said. We all four were on our knees, digging like dogs burying bones at the place where Agnes had indicated. We hit something solid.

"Easy," Agnes said. "Don't damage it."

Carefully she went along the dimensions of the root with the knife, prying here and there. We all dug again. Agnes began to wrestle the root out. It was a huge thing, shaped like a deformed giant coconut. She handed the knife back to Ruby after wiping it over the grass to clean it. She banged the root several times, knocking off the dirt. She took out a pocketknife and opened the blade with her teeth. Then she cut the root hairs off.

"Over here," she said.

We all followed her to a rock that was partially in the creek. She plunged the root into the water and washed it. When that was done, she set it on the rock. She and Ruby began talking to it in Cree. July was staring, and I could see she was racked with fear. The incantation, or whatever it was, lasted for several minutes. Agnes again opened the knife blade with her teeth.

"My whittling knife," she said.

She began cutting the root in long lateral strokes. She worked intently and with great deliberation. Then there began to be a strange recklessness in this activity. I started to ask a question, but Ruby warned me off by cupping her hand over my mouth. The root was beginning to take shape, but it was too soon to tell what it was. Now Agnes was bearing down in certain places with the knife blade. She picked at the shaved pieces and then held it up for inspection. It resembled a crude horse, about a foot in length.

Ruby ran her hand over the carved root. "You are a tolerable artist, Agnes," she said. "The terrible powers of the blood are emerging."

Agnes took a few more swipes with her pocketknife and then etched some symbols on the neck.

We heard the whine of tires over the gravel road. A truck went by, going the other way. Everyone ducked low.

"That's him," Ruby whispered. "I could smell him a mile away."

My heart started palpitating and I was hugging July, who was as horrified as I was. Agnes ran and got her medicine bundle from the truck bed and came back. She unrolled it on the rock. She found a small crystal, picked up a rock, and hammered it into the head of the horse figure. The protruding crystal made the carving look like a unicorn. The sky was becoming overcast with dark purple clouds. A loud clap of thunder rolled between the cliffs and echoed over our heads. Lightning squiggled through the clouds. A sprinkle of rain immediately followed.

July ran to the truck and brought back several pieces of canvas that had been cut into rain ponchos. We were soaked by the time we got them on.

Agnes shaved off a small piece of the root and handed it to me. "Eat," she said. "Lightning root to conquer your enemy. Eat what he eats."

She passed a small shaving to July and one to Ruby, then ate one herself. The root tasted very bitter, but I swallowed it. I thought it might make me nauseated, but the feeling soon went away.

"Your hand," she ordered.

I held it out for her. She punctured the tip of my index finger with the small blade of her pocketknife. I jumped and tried to suck it, but she restrained me. She squeezed out a large drop of blood.

"Remember that a woman's blood has more power than a man's," she said. "Now make a lightning mark on the flank of the carved horse."

I did so, painting a zigzag with my finger.

Agnes pierced her finger and put a lightning symbol next to mine. July and Ruby did the same on the other side of the horse figure. Agnes then tied a piece of what looked like eagle fluff and something else I could not see around the belly of the root creature.

"It's about time," Ruby said.

"It's finished," Agnes said.

We walked to the road, and Agnes told the three of us to stay hidden in the reeds and watch. This we did. Ruby's face was impassive, but I was chewing my bottom lip nervously. Agnes, bent low to the ground, snaked her way to the edge of the road. She hid behind the black and gnarled trunk of an oak tree. In her crude poncho she was virtually unnoticeable.

Five or ten minutes went by. All of us were crouched low in the rain. We heard the chugging of a truck engine. The lights were on and beamed down the road, though it wasn't dark. I felt wet and clammy and miserable, and I didn't know what was going on. The fine rain was sheeting down with such density that I could barely see Agnes or even the tree she was behind.

Just before the black pickup rolled by, Agnes leapt out from behind the tree trunk. She yelled some word I didn't recognize and threw what I guessed to be the carved horse figure. It landed with a thud in the open bed of the pickup. A roll of thunder shook the ground, and the pickup began to swerve and fishtail down the slippery road. Three lightning bolts split the sky. I did not know whether to run, stay put, or die of anxiety.

I had visions of Red Dog coming after us with a club and bludgeoning us to death. But what happened was right out of a slapstick comedy movie. The truck continued to weave and skid out of control. It hit a huge rut sideways and flipped up on two wheels, screeching across the road on its side. Red Dog, Ben, and Drum leapt out of the now-topside door. They looked around, eyes filled with the most gruesome kind of shock. Red Dog screamed, and Ben and Drum joined him. They ran pell-mell in three different directions.

"You would have thought their pants were on fire," I exclaimed to Ruby.

"Worse," Ruby commented.

Agnes appeared and said, "Let's get out of here."

We quickly piled into the truck. July's pickup flashed by Red Dog just as she hit high gear. I looked back, and his eyes were filled with terror. He cut across a ditch, still running at full speed, still screaming.

Agnes and Ruby elbowed each other and laughed for the next twenty miles.

"He won't bother us for a while," Agnes said.

I started to inquire about the strange root carving, but then thought better of it. If Agnes wanted me to know, she would tell me.

The rain slacked off. Ruby insisted we take a detour from our normal route in order to visit a place where the fishing was extraordinary.

7

The Sacred Clown

"Are you lost, Ruby?" Agnes asked irritably.

"It's here somewhere. I know it is. Can I help it if I'm blind?"

We had bounced over one rutted road after another while Ruby looked for her fishing spot. Then she asked July to stop, and she listened intently and tested the air currents with her fingers.

"You'll be glad when you taste the trout," she said.

It had been raining earlier, but the sky had cleared to a rich turquoise blue. The storm had washed the air and trees clean. Every leaf and blade of grass sparkled in the afternoon sun. It was warm and the air was pungent with the aroma of freshly bathed earth.

"Here it is," Ruby shouted. "Over there. Right there."

We turned off the road and went several hundred yards.

"Park under those trees, July," Ruby ordered, sniffing the air like a bloodhound.

July drove to a flat area and parked under a stand of cottonwood trees. We all got out and walked down to the river. Ruby and July were carrying fly rods and tackle boxes.

"This is the place, right here." Ruby was smiling broadly.

Beavers had dammed up one narrow place, and the result was a large pond exactly as Ruby had described it.

"I've been coming here since I was a little girl," Ruby cried happily. "This was my grandpa's special fishing hole," she said, flattening her hand just above the water to feel the ripples. "I'm glad I brought enough fishing tackle for all of us."

She sat down on a large fallen tree that extended into the water. Low waves of backwater lapped against the shoreline. It looked shallow, and I could see the dark shadows of rocks under the surface of the water. Ruby was testing her lines and checking the reels. She turned toward me.

"Well, don't just stand there. Go catch some crickets and dig some worms. You can't fish without bait."

Watching her a moment longer, I marveled at how she could possibly do all that she did and be utterly blind. She was deftly tying a hook to a leader and putting sinkers on the line.

"Don't worry, Lynn," she said. "I won't hook myself. I could do this with my eyes closed. Now git."

Not wanting to catch crickets or dig worms, I went to the pickup and took out the camp stove and the cooking utensils we would need to cook our catch, if we had any.

Agnes and July made a game of catching grasshoppers. July would fan the clump-grass and herd them toward Agnes, who stood laughing and grabbing at the insects. Agnes placed the captured bugs in a Mason jar.

A warm wind came up from the west, and I was mesmerized by the soft rustle in the tree branches overhead. I took out a sleeping bag and unrolled it on the ground. The wind had a song. I realized how thankful I was for her music. I laid down, closed my eyes, and listened. It was such a pleasant sensation that I could not get up and pull myself away. I fell into a reverie of dreams. I had the sensation that the wind was alive. I wanted to pull the gentle trilling sound into my mouth and take her inside.

"Are you eating the west wind again?" Ruby snorted at me. "Leave some for us."

I sat up, startled. "But I didn't mean . . ." My voice trailed off.

"Come on, Sleeping Beauty. Let's go fishing." She kicked me with the soft toe of her desert boot.

I got up hurriedly. Ruby had turned and was halfway to the shoreline. July and Agnes had already baited their hooks and were standing in different spots on the shore, casting out into the middle of the pond. As I walked up beside Ruby, she turned and held a squirming night-crawler up in my face.

"Here," she said. "Bait your hook."

I took the worm. She sat down and I joined her. I had fished avidly with my father as a child, but I had not baited a hook in twenty years.

The worm had a slimy feeling. "Why can't we tie flies instead?" I complained, holding the wriggling body gingerly between my finger and thumb.

Ruby was annoyed by the question. "Because we're using live bait, that's why. You know about bait, don't you? You ought to. You've been Red Dog's bait for years now." She shoved a rod at me and carefully placed the hook between the fingers of my other hand. She cocked her head sideways in a birdlike way. "Come now, Lynn. That worm is part of the giveaway for the fish. Soon we will be worm food. It will happen before you know it. Don't be selfish. Don't cheat the worm of his destiny any more than he would cheat you of yours."

Very slowly and with much distaste, I threaded the worm on the hook. The act made me feel queasy.

"I know life is predatory, Ruby, but it still bothers me."

"We are each the food for our brothers and sisters. Whether we are hungry wolves, fish, or the wind, we all devour one another and become transformed. Your problem is that you get caught in believing the dream. You get too close to what you are looking at, and you miss the greater vision. You forget the dreamer. There is a warrior trout out there in the river who has spent his whole life preparing for this combat. It's his destiny and yours. When you meet your trout, honor the power of that moment and give way to the magnitude of your destiny with him."

She regarded me doubtfully and then stood up. She went to a tree stump that had fallen in the water. With a new determination I picked up my rod and followed her. I saw a nearby place where the water was flowing over a boulder, making a small rapids, boiling around in circles and pockets of crystalline swirls.

"Watch me," Ruby said. She flipped back her pole and cast her bait out into the middle of the channel before the river flowed out to fill the pond. In a moment she had a bite and reeled in a twelve-inch trout.

"Now you try," she said. She put the wiggling trout on a stringer and rebaited her hook.

Further down the bank, Agnes and July were having no luck. I cast my bait out into the water and slowly started to reel in the line, keeping it taut. It was good sport, but I had no bites. Ruby cast out again and immediately got a hit. Laughing, she reeled in another large trout.

We fished for more than an hour. Agnes and July were thoroughly frustrated. None of us had caught anything except Ruby, who got several browns and rainbows. She had also thrown back at least a half dozen smaller ones. In exasperation the three of us gathered around her.

"All right, Ruby," Agnes said, frowning. "What's your secret? What are we doing wrong?"

"Wrong? Why, nothing. The secret is luck, of course. But you have to learn how to make your own luck good."

Agnes was standing with her hands on her hips, glaring at Ruby. "And how do we do that?"

"What's it worth to you? You know an angler's secrets are more precious than gold. And greatly protected. Why should I tell any of you? What have you ever done for me that I should share such a closely guarded secret?"

"Ruby!" we all shouted in unison. "Tell us what you're doing to catch so many fish."

"Well, okay, ladies," she said, slapping her hands together with glee. "Watch carefully, and I'll show you a real fisherman's little secret." Waving her arm and showing us there was nothing up her sleeve, she took a plug of chewing tobacco out of her pocket. She bit off a piece and worked it in her mouth for several minutes. "Now watch this," she said, still chewing. "This is called magnetizing the hook." She held up the hook and spit tobacco juice on it. "This always works. Spit on it.

Spit is spirit. With tobacco it's a mixture of substance and spirit that gives the hook good luck. The harmony of substance and spirit always brings luck. Never forget it. And if the hook has good luck, so do you." She handed me the plug of tobacco. "You first, Lynn."

"Okay," I said. "If you say so. But I've never chewed tobacco before. I'll probably get sick." I chewed a small nibble. It was sweet and burned my tongue. Then I spat on my fishing hook just as Ruby had done. July and Agnes were doing likewise.

Ruby cast out into a hollow in the river. "See those pockets?" she said as we were all baiting our hooks with worms. "Those swirling places."

We all acknowledged that we saw them.

Ruby's line hardened. She made a sharp jerk and began reeling. "Out there. Those are the resting places of the trout. If you can cast into those watery bowls, the fish will always eat, because they're hungry and tired."

We all separated, stationing ourselves at various places along the bank. We were looking for those water pockets Ruby had described. As each of us found one, we each cast out with renewed hope. July had a hit, and then Agnes. They both pulled in large, fighting trout. Finally, my line jerked. I thought I had a whale and was very excited. When I reeled it in, it was very small, about six inches. Agnes and July were laughing and pointing at my disappointing little fish. Ruby came over and knelt down beside me as I was endeavoring to take it off the hook. She placed her fingers lightly on the flapping trout.

"See," she said. "You are face-to-face with your own destiny. But she is still young, a child fish. Let her grow and come back here next year. Perhaps then it will be time to eat her."

Ruby handed me the fish. I threw her back. She hit the water with a flourish and then went deep. Ruby left, and I sat for a while, watching the water lap against the shore.

Ruby held up a full stringer. We decided we had enough fish. The shadows were slanting out across the plains. The clear golden sunlight etched the mountain range around us into an Olympian resting place fit for ancient gods. It was a perfect time for dinner.

We cleaned the fish along the shore, shucking the guts out and leaving the entrails for the beavers. We built a fire and sat on our sleeping bags. We had an old-fashioned fish fry beneath the towering gilt spires of the Canadian Rockies. After cleaning up the dinner dishes, we went down to the water's edge. We said prayers to the spirit of the fish and left tobacco and corn pollen.

I awoke before dawn to the smell of pine smoke from the campfire. Ruby and Agnes were up, warming their hands and talking. July was breathing rhythmically, curled up inside her sleeping bag. My own bag was moist, and the ground was wet with dew. The stars were still out. I saw the bare outlines of the green-sloped mountains where the sun was about to come up. I could hear the surging dark water of the river washing against the banks.

As the sunlight shafted over the crest of the mountain peaks, I shared some fried bread and leftover fish with Agnes and Ruby. We finished the last of a jar of homemade blackberry preserves. Noting that we needed supplies, I offered to take the truck to the nearest town and get some staples.

I left camp with my list of provisions and drove off down the dusty road. A half hour later I chugged into a small town. It was a quaint little place surrounded by green fields. I could see the hills and mountains beyond. I found a secondhand store where I thought I might be able to buy a heavy sweater. It was down a back street, behind the hardware store and the grocery store, the town's two major commercial enterprises. It was difficult to maneuver the truck. It took all my strength to cut the corner and get the huge pickup into a parking place. My shoulder and arm muscles were burning as I turned off the ignition. I scooted across the front seat and opened the passenger door.

Through the big plate-glass window, the inside of the store looked gloomy. I went up the few steps, entered, and was greeted by a musty smell. The front of the store was filled with all sorts of secondhand appliances.

"Hello," I called.

No one answered. Toward the back of the store were long racks of used clothing and shelves of old paperback books. I can never pass up a shelf of books. A half hour had gone by, and I was reading an old book of interviews by Pauline Kael.

"Oh, you startled me," I said. I was looking into the brown face of a young woman standing in front of me. I had thought the store was deserted.

The woman asked if she could help me. I bought several books, and we ended up talking about her Cree grandparents in Montana. I tried on a yellow cardigan, and she insisted that I take it as a gift. It was just what I wanted, so I accepted it without much protest. I handed her a hawk feather I had in my pocket, which I had picked up while we were fishing. She told me her name was Shirley and I told her mine. We hugged when I finally left, and I had a very warm feeling about the young woman.

I went to the market, wearing the ribbed yellow sweater, and got two boxes of provisions. With some difficulty I swung the unwieldy pickup truck out of the parking place and drove back to our campsite. I felt wonderful. I rolled down the window and gulped in the dry, pine-scented fresh air. No one even looked up as I parked the truck. I had bought some sandwiches and I gave one each to July, Ruby, and Agnes. Agnes looked at me very intensely. She took the sandwich and laid it down without even looking at it. She started picking at my sweater.

"Nice," she said. "I've never seen that before. Where did you get it?"

"I met the nicest girl named Shirley in the secondhand store where I bought a bunch of books. Her grandmother is related to—"

Agnes interrupted me in a harsh tone. "So, where did you get the sweater?"

I was taken aback. "Ah . . . Shirley gave it to me."

Then Ruby started picking at my sleeve. "Nice sweater," she said, her face in a pout. "Nobody ever gives me presents like that."

Agnes looked angry and distressed. "I'll never be able to give you enough if people keep giving you presents like this."

"Hey, you can have the sweater. Better still, I'll go get one for each of you. What's the matter with you two?" I asked, distressed.

Agnes shook her head dejectedly. "I'll just never be able to keep up with all these other people giving you things."

"Agnes," I said, my voice rising. "Shirley gave me a nice sweater out of the kindness of her heart. What's wrong with that? I didn't think you needed a sweater."

"I don't need a sweater," she shouted. "But my grandchildren need sweaters. They're not fortunate like you. People just give you things out of the blue."

A miserable feeling began to steal over me. It was as if my warm affection for Agnes and Ruby were being pierced. I was deeply hurt and completely dejected. I did not understand how the gift of a sweater could so completely affront them. Agnes was walking around in a circle. She kicked the camp stove over on its side. She was angry and very old-looking.

"Even this filthy stove is out of gas," Agnes yelled. "White gas is expensive, and we don't have any more money."

Ruby was picking at my sweater again. Her lips were pursed, and she was pinching me.

"I'll go get some gas," I offered.

"No," Agnes said abruptly. "You don't understand. I can't go get gas. You and I are not in the same place in life. You're a successful white woman. I'm just an Indian. Nobody understands us Indians. Everything has been taken from us. I don't have a real family. My husband is dead and so is my daughter. And I'm flat-assed broke. Look at that dilapidated truck I have to go around in. It's a piece of junk. I want to get a Porsche, but I'll never be able to have one. But you could have one. You're just in a different world from me. The cops would probably arrest an old Indian woman driving a fancy Porsche, but they wouldn't arrest you. And now you come back with a brand-new sweater!"

"It's a secondhand sweater, Agnes."

"That doesn't matter," she shouted. "It's the principle that matters."

"Yeah," Ruby said. She shoved me a bit, not hard, but enough to move me a little. "I feel like one of your maids. There's always something coming between us—your work, your books, having to make money. How can we ever be together?" She kicked her sleeping bag in a heap. "And look at this sleeping bag. All greasy. Even has holes in it. I can't replace it, either. I have no money. Who's going to give an old Indian woman money? I may as well be dead as be different. I hate being different."

"You're not different, Ruby," I said. Tears were rolling down my cheeks. "You're special."

"Well, I'm tired of being special. I wish I were a white woman like you. And I'm even blind. Old, Indian, and blind. That's a winning combination, isn't it?" She was hobbling around as if she were an antique, and her hands were shaking.

"What's all this talk about money?" I asked. "I always ask you if you need money."

"We don't need money!" Ruby cried loudly. "We want success. We want to be remembered for something like you will be remembered."

"What do you mean *like me*?" My voice was high-pitched and out of control. "I'm just a dumb person coming to you for teaching, as your friend."

"How do I know that you don't say that to other Indians? Maybe you don't really care about me. Maybe you're just using me." Ruby paused and straightened up indignantly. "Hmph. After all I've done for you."

I fought back the tears. "But I love you."

She turned on me angrily. "How do I know that? I've been cheated and lied to so much by all the people I've ever loved. How can I trust you? You're so secretive anyway."

"But you taught me to be secretive."

"That doesn't matter," Ruby said. "Maybe I was wrong."

"Nope," said Agnes, waving her hand. "I can't trust you because you're in a different place in life. Ruby and I are just Indians. We're misfits. We know a lot, sure. But nobody will pay us for that knowledge. So what good is it? We live like a couple of old hoboes, like vagabonds."

"You do not. I've never known anyone so extraordinary and beautiful." I was weeping.

July finished her sandwich. She had been sitting some distance away on a pebbly flat area by the river, and now she approached to within a few yards away. She said, "What's up?"

She caught sight of me and stopped dead in her tracks. She saw that I was crying and that Agnes and Ruby looked upset. She came up and put her arm around me. "Nice sweater," she said.

"Well, if you want it, you can have it," I cried. "I don't want the damned thing anyway."

July jerked back, stunned by my reply. "No, Lynn. Honest. I don't need your sweater." She looked around sheepishly.

"Don't give me one of your miserable looks," Agnes snapped. "You couldn't possibly understand, July. You're young and I'm old. I'm just an old beat-up loser, and you have your whole life ahead of you. You and I are in different worlds. You can never really share anything with me."

"I didn't do anything," July said frantically. "So I'm young. What does that have to do with it?"

"Be quiet, July," Ruby scolded. "Are you happy because I'm old and blind? Agnes is broke, and it's all your fault. Yes, you. You and Lynn. It's all your fault for humoring Agnes and me."

Both Agnes and Ruby stomped around the campsite, raging. Each of them yelled out examples of their scorn. Everything was wrong. The camp was dirty. They were without money. Their parents had destroyed their lives. They dwelled on being old and in pain and not white. There was an endless tirade of insults at me and July for being "different." The whole performance was insane, but by the end of a half hour, July and I were both sobbing uncontrollably.

"Everything was fine until you got here wearing that obnoxious sweater," Ruby said. "Why don't you just get the hell out of here until the wind changes?"

"What do you mean?" I asked, still racked with sobs.

Agnes pulled me up and led me to the truck. She dangled the keys in front of me. "Take them. Maybe you better go. And then drive in again. We'll start over."

"Yes. Leave," Ruby ordered. "Come back and maybe you'll be in a better mood."

"Me?" I said. "Are you serious?"

"Yes, go," Agnes demanded. "Come back again if you feel like it."

Sniveling, I got into the truck and started the engine. I wanted to say something, but Agnes and Ruby were waving for me to go. I drove off down the road thinking I would like to go and find Shirley and get drunk. My eyes still brimmed with tears. I put on the brakes and stopped. I wasn't going to be shoved out of the nest by those two old women. I backed up and turned around. When I got to the campsite, I pulled in slowly, not really wanting to be there.

I got out of the truck. My eyes darted around. I felt like a turtle in its shell. With every paranoid step I expected Agnes's wrath to descend on me. I noticed the camp was swept and picked up. Agnes, Ruby, and July were sitting down by the river. They waved at me. Their faces were beaming. I hesitantly approached them. They rose to greet me.

"Hi, Lynn," Agnes said. "Really good sandwiches. Thanks so much."

"Yeah, thanks," Ruby piped in.

"That was the best sandwich," July agreed. "There must have been three kinds of meat in it. And they weren't stingy with the cheese, either."

Their faces were all smiling and pleasant.

"That's a becoming sweater, Lynn. Is it new?" Agnes asked. I hesitated, but she encouraged me to answer. "Tell me about it."

"Yes, well . . ." And I went through the whole story.

This time Agnes was very interested in Shirley, and so were Ruby and July.

"That yellow is a lovely color on you, Lynn," Ruby said. "You should wear it often."

Agnes put her arm around me, and we sat down on a ledge leading up to the campsite. Her eyes were animated. She told me how wonderful it was that I had found my way into their circle and how we had enhanced each other's lives. She talked about the difficulties of being Indian, and how she and Ruby had chosen to come into this earthwalk as Indian women to learn about the problems and challenges that the situation presented to them. She talked for a long time, and her words were soothing.

Ruby began to speak. Instead of being angry about her truly difficult position in life, Ruby talked about how being raped and blinded at an early age had actually brought her into the medicine world. When she was a young girl, she had lived with her grandfather. She was alone one day when four white surveyors happened on the cabin. They saw Ruby. She was so beautiful and vulnerable. They raped her, and then they blinded her so she could not identify them. Her life was ruined. She wanted to die. A medicine man named Four Deers, in the north, saved her and taught her deer medicine. He had opened gateways to perception that she would never have explored had she lived a normal life. Because of her blindness, she had developed extrasensory abilities that were remarkable, to say the least.

"It's so wonderful," Agnes said, "to be able to travel and camp like this. To be in the last vestiges of wilderness left in the world. So few people have the opportunity to enjoy this sacred earth." Her smile was genuine.

"What about being broke and old?" I asked tentatively.

"I'm not broke. Who said that? Where money is concerned, we have you to take care of us."

Ruby chuckled and Agnes joined her.

"We have everything we need," Agnes went on. "If we don't have white gas, we'll build a fire. And if the truck breaks down, we'll just go find Arion or hitchhike. We can fish for food and live off the land. There's plenty out here to sustain life. Besides, we have the opportunity to teach you, and that makes us rich."

Ruby squeezed next to me on the ledge. They both hugged me. Beautiful July, as graceful as a deer, stood nearby, watching this display of unaccustomed affection.

"Sit down here next to me, July," Agnes said. The four of us sat together in a row with our arms around each other. We were silent, but I was feeling much better.

"A little while ago you thought you had driven into hell," Agnes said. I nodded my head in agreement. Agnes continued, "I was negative and pessimistic and dark. All I could see were the bad aspects of my life. I separated myself by my attitude and created a very lonely broken country, a hard place to be. Ruby and I did this in order to show you that your world is exactly as you create it. You can choose to see nothing but darkness and pain. Surely it is there and needs to be acknowledged. But not in a negative way. If there is no gas, you go earn money to get gas. Or you change the pathway and find heat from another source. I don't know if you noticed, but the wind shook and went crazy when all that was happening. I was locked in an outpouring of negativity that poisoned the atmosphere around me. No matter what you said or did, it would have been wrong, because I was behind the shadow barrier that neither you nor I could climb. Many people are trapped in that place of pain. Beware. It marks your burial, the death of your dreams, and the beginning of sorrows."

We all stood, climbed up the embankment, and walked ahead toward the truck. I stopped Agnes by pulling on her arm. "But what if I'm positive? I felt great when I drove in. What if other people like you are negative and they lay it on you?"

"Then ask yourself," she said, "why that is happening. Why did you choose to be with that person at this time in life? And can that person grow? Or is that person hopelessly trapped in his or her own pessimism? You are a warrioress, a hunter. You take life's circumstances as a challenge. What can you learn from that mirror? And can you teach that person a better way? If not, perhaps you should cut out and head down trails that are more fruitful. Don't allow anyone to ruin the happy hunting territories of your own mind. A happy frame of mind is your food. Protect her. Go where there is fresh grass and clear water. Where the game is plentiful to hunt."

"What if someone insults you and hurts you?" I asked.

"A warrioress always needs a challenge. Why is it that a person is able to insult you? What's going on with your misdirected pride? If we blow ourselves up in this manner, we are meat for any insult. But if we are not puffed up with pride, very little can hurt us." She laughed. "Besides, with no false pride, you are a smaller target."

"Sometimes I can't help being negative. Then what?" I was still feeling foolish for having been tricked by Agnes's charade.

"Observe your own behavior. Look down on yourself like a noble eagle in the sky. See how foolish you are, and forgive yourself. You are only human. See what the thunder-chiefs see. Against the grandeur of the sky, we all shrink in importance."

I realized the extent of my own negativity and felt very stupid at having been tricked so well. While Agnes and I had talked, Ruby had been rummaging around in the boxes of groceries. She was using her buck knife to open a can of pears. She slipped and sliced her finger on the raw edge of the protruding tin. Blood trickled down her hand.

"Look at this," she said. "Wasn't that stupid?"

I went up to her. "Ruby, you've cut yourself."

"I'll live," Ruby said, holding up her bleeding finger. "But what's the matter with you? You act like someone hit you in the back of the head with a two-by-four."

"I'm upset that I couldn't tell you were tricking me. I feel so stupid."

"I'm counting on you to wise up one of these days, Lynn," Ruby said. "The path of knowledge stings sometimes. It is not an effortless pursuit. Sometimes you get cut and bruised, or even broken. But when you find yourself wounded, that is not the time to feel guilty. Wouldn't you think it was inappropriate if I cut off my finger because I sliced it here?"

"Yes, I would."

"Feeling guilty about your own weakness and failures is as abusive as that. It's like amputating my finger because it's sore and because I've done something stupid like cut myself. Do you see?"

"Yes," I said. "I do. It's a good lesson."

"Here's another one," Ruby said. She shifted her position to my side. She spit on her cut finger, cupped her hand over it, and rubbed it. Then she pulled the same finger out and showed it to me. There was no cut or mark. The wound had completely healed or disappeared. I wondered if I had been tricked again.

"How on earth did you do that, Ruby?"

"It's unimportant. The important thing is that I didn't punish myself unnecessarily."

Once again I had been jarred out of my normal state.

8

The Life and Death Ghost Dolls

In the early morning light, I was scrubbing the cast iron skillet with steel wool, immersing it in the river water. I had seen a white-tailed deer grazing on meadow grass and a red-tailed hawk circling above. The bird, with its great wingspan, seemed to be traveling near me, checking me out.

Barefooted, Agnes was wading and splashing water on her face. Her long salt-and-pepper hair was loose. She dried her face with an old, faded bandana handkerchief, then used it to tie back her hair. She sat down next to me and put on her boots.

"How do I look?" she asked.

"You look super," I said with enthusiasm.

"Good," she said. "An old coyote can still look formidable."

"Are you an old coyote, Agnes?"

"More coyote than you know, and older than you might think possible."

"Well, you don't look like a coyote, and you don't look very old, either."

She adjusted her silver concho belt. When she looked at me, there was a certain mockery in her eyes—at least, that's what I thought it was. Perhaps it was simple amusement. She pulled a dark shawl around her shoulders.

By and by she spoke. "The other day at the top of Elk Horn Mountain, I said we would have a feast and celebration honoring your inward sun. The time seems pretty good. Before we leave this camp, I want you to prepare for this celebration by accomplishing one more task. The fact that Red Dog is dogging your trail makes me realize the importance of this next step. Come on."

We walked along the river, as it meandered and snaked through the valley. The wind picked up and blew in from the west. We went along the river's edge, walking over the flat river stones that were gray like a squirrel's hide. Lacy shadow patterns were thrown delicately onto the sandy banks by the cottonwoods towering overhead.

"Lynn, it is good that you have held council with your ancestor father within you. The lights around your heart have brightened and have found a good home."

Agnes paused for a moment after the two of us had rounded a turn in the river. As we walked along, she picked up feathers, pieces of dry grass, sticks, and other things. She asked me to pick up anything that especially pulled me or caught my eye.

"Do you remember the feelings you had when you thought of your father?" Agnes asked. She indicated a wide sandy beach, and we sat down once more. She placed all of our found objects between us and took out her pocketknife.

"Yes, I remember." The recollection filled me with a nameless apprehension and a dark sensation zipped up my spine. I suddenly felt like a clock that was wound too tight. I felt a slight pain in my chest and shoulders. I bent forward, hollowed my body, and shrugged my shoulders forward. My hands held each of my arms at the upper muscles.

Agnes reached over and shook me briskly. "Loosen up," she said. "Your whole body is trailing after your emotions."

I tried to sit more erect.

"Your emotions deform you, Lynn. It is not in the medicine way to let this happen. It is not free. It is not good. You must make your *heava* sit up and take notice. Let your *heava* know you are no longer going to tolerate it."

"And how am I supposed to do that?"

"I have often told you that your inside moon lodge is equivalent to your outside sun lodge. The moon is more powerful than the sun.

In its passivity, it overwhelms the world and becomes only light. Have you ever heard of ghost dolls?"

"Not that I remember. What are they? And why are they called ghost dolls?"

"They are called ghost dolls because they are attached to you. That is, you force a part of your spirit to animate them."

"I suppose you are going to tell me to make one of these dolls."

"No. I am going to tell you to make two of them. You will begin with a mourner doll."

"A mourner doll?"

"A mourner doll is you. It contains within its belly all your pain, greed, sorrow, and fears. In other words, it is a doll built and divined as a tangible expression of your intangible addictions. It is made of your crazy winds, your negativity, the impulses that have crippled your spirit. A mourner doll is your death. It is made for your transformation from one life to another. It is a conveyance, a canoe, a bridge. It becomes a symbol on the altar of your metamorphosis from your immature self-lodge to your medicine lodge, where your sacred things are kept in this lifetime. One of these sacred items is the bone-keeper doll, the second one you will make. It represents your life. The spirit lives in your bones. It holds your good intentions, the things that you want to accomplish in this lifetime. Your spiritual and earth-plane goals are part of the body of the bone-keeper doll."

"But why are they ghost dolls, Agnes?"

"Because they exist like shadows of your spirit, reminding you of your inner life."

"Sort of like fetishes?" I thought of the inspired carvings called fetishes and the wrapped and feathered objects that some Indigenous people made to represent various states of mind.

"Yes, these dolls represent the powers within you. Your life power and your death power. What you choose not to look at in life rules your life. That is why the mourner doll is so important, and why I want you to make her first. Fashion her out of the darkest depths within your own spirit. Build her of your twisted and broken dreams, the things you want to bury and be done with forever. The mourner doll represents your death and a process of mourning for what is about to die."

Agnes had been absently whittling on a piece of driftwood that was full of ugly burls. It was on the sand next to us, and I had not paid much attention. Now she tied it with grass and feathers. "Something like this," she said, holding up the doll-like form. It had a grim and forbidding look. She waved it in front of my face, then set it back down on the sand next to her.

"It makes me feel unsettled," I said.

"Well, it should. This is the first doll for you to make. Then make the bone-keeper doll second." She sifted sand through her fingers, holding her hand up to the wind and letting the grains blow gently away. "Listen to your inner voice, your deepest voice, and you will know how to proceed. Remember that the bone-keeper represents your hopes and future accomplishments."

I nodded that I understood. She stood me up and walked around me in a circle several times. She began to pray softly in Cree. Then she smudged me and blessed me with sweetgrass smoke. She pushed her hand on my solar plexus lightly, four times. Then she said, "Get to work."

I watched the wind blow her skirt and loosely tied-back hair as she walked back to the bend in the river and disappeared, leaving me to my task. First I decided to make a medicine circle out of the river stones. Then I blessed it with tobacco and cornmeal and entered the circle from the east, closing off the entrance with tobacco. I sat in the center, facing west, and said prayers to the Great Spirit and Mother Earth. Then I contemplated the powers of the west, which are the sacred dream, death and rebirth, and introspection. I tried to look at my own form in terms of death and my twisted nature. I looked at Crazy Woman inside of me and watched her tugging at my sanity. I thought of my father again and released myself to that old sadness that I had given away. After experiencing all of those emotions, I left the medicine wheel and began searching through the vast wilderness terrain for any article that represented the various levels of feelings within me. The riverbeds and fields were abundant. I found old, greasy feathers and parts of a dead bird, its feet curled and grotesque. I used an old burlap potato sack left by campers to carry the feathers and dead bird parts, along with a small bleached vertebra, sticks with odd, spooky twists, and many other items that spoke to me of my *heava*. I gathered them all and went back to my medicine wheel. I prayed there and cried. I talked with these objects and began to give birth to a form. I concentrated on my solar plexus and the intent of my will. I took out my pocketknife and began whittling and carving a foot-long piece of driftwood. The old gray wood was seasoned by the turbulent river, but it was soft and easily shaped. I became fascinated by the way a crooked and bent shape was beginning to emerge from the wood. It was as if she had always been lying dormant within the structure of the wood, waiting to be unfurled and set free.

When the mourner finally emerged, her dark power was apparent. She was a true katchina, a spirit doll of my own misgivings. I made small medicine bags of things precious to me, taking my hair, a drop of blood, and spit, and combined them, placing the bags on the belly, back, and heart of the doll. She was grotesquely wonderful. To look at her, no one could mistake that she was of my *heava*. When finally I was finished, I wrapped her in a piece of burlap cut from the potato sack and set her in front of the west stone of the wheel.

I turned and faced east, toward illumination. I let my mind move into my goals for the future and precisely how I wanted to order my destiny. As I sat there, I felt the west wind pushing against my back as though it were supporting my efforts and had come to encourage me. I contemplated the magnificence of this life. I saw more clearly than I ever had that we are all exactly in the position in life that we choose to be in, no more or less. We are not victims of circumstance. We have formed our own circumstance for many complex reasons, which often remain unnamed out of our own ignorance or our inability to learn and face the truth.

I left the medicine wheel through the east door and began searching for fibers, stones, mica, wood, bones, and anything that would properly reflect the joyousness of my spirit. I was astonished at how different my search was this time. When I looked for the *heava* pieces, I had projected a dark and lifeless feeling onto everything. There had been an unnatural silence around me, and I had felt a separation between myself and nature. Walking down the riverbed, I saw different aspects in the same things I had seen before. Stones that reflected the light caught my eye. On the flat land on the top of one ridge, I found an anthill. I had seen it previously but had not realized that there were tiny seed crystals placed on the outside of the hill, crystals that the ants had brought up from the depths of their *kivas*, their sacred rooms underground. I collected them with great care.

I threaded my way through small clumps of bushes and out onto a flat meadow. Instinctively, I moved toward higher ground. At last I found a long shinbone from a deer who had spent her last moments among a grove of trees with beautiful foliage. I sensed that the deer had been female and that she had been surprised by a bobcat. For a moment I saw her hopeless battle and fear, and then her chosen death. Life is a struggle, and then we die. The deer died instantly of a broken neck, her last breath of sage-scented air that had come from the north. I picked up the bone. It vibrated between my fingers, and I knew I had remembered her spirit correctly. I knelt down for a moment, sending a prayer to the house of the deer spirits. I smoothed the earth where I had found the bone. I left an offering of cornmeal and burned a small piece of sage.

I returned to the medicine wheel and sat in the center. I arranged all of the objects that I had found in front of me. Then I picked up the deer bone, got out my pocketknife again, and began to carve. There was no question about it. This was the perfect armature for my bone-keeper doll. I tied several stick bundles and feathers along the sides, using strings from the burlap potato sack. I put a large mussel shell at the neck. I fashioned two legs from a V-shaped piece of wood and attached them with clay and twine. There were even protuberances that looked like feet. I etched in toes with my knife. I made two arms from smaller bones that extended to bird-claw fingers. I used a small, weathered gourd for the head and face. I cut enough of my own hair to make a sort of wig and attached it by punching small perforations in the top of the gourd and tying loops of hair through the holes. I wedged mica along the forehead and cheeks. I made an oval mouth and stained the lips with berries. Next, I bound white and brown feathers and stuck them on the top of her head. I rubbed some of my own blood into several strands of my hair, which I then twined around her neck. I smeared white clay and river mud on areas of her face. I braided some flaxen grass shoots and hung a tiny medicine bag from it. It contained the anthill crystals. The doll was a warrioress, so I built a bow from a small piece of limber cottonwood and strung it with some fibers of burlap. I made arrows and hung them on her back by braided grass thongs. Then I painted her all over with red berry juice and feathered her with bits of fluff I had found caught on a bush. When I was done, I wrapped her, too, in a piece of burlap.

It was afternoon when I had begun. Now long shadows bent down the arroyos near me. I took deep breaths of air so dry it singed my nostrils. I reveled in the crispness that stiffened the blue denim next to my skin. I felt the proximity of the source of pure water, and it awakened my body down to the core. Night was descending fast. The sky was pallid and pearl-gray stars were emerging. They began to blink. The crickets were singing, and the frogs were croaking from the riverbanks. I heard a brisk rustling of bushes from behind me. I turned, startled to find Agnes and Ruby approaching with armfuls of dried branches.

"You two scared me," I said.

"Well, since you didn't send up any smoke signals, we thought we better come and find you," Agnes said.

They dumped the wood on the ground, and Agnes began breaking it into short pieces to build a fire. She spent several minutes arranging the kindling and placing the larger wood. When it met with her satisfaction, she lit it. She scolded and blew her breath on it until the fire caught and licked with flames.

Leading me by the hand, Ruby placed me in the south of the medicine wheel, the seat of my little girl shield. Agnes placed the two ghost dolls in front of me and told me to unwrap them. When this was done, Ruby positioned the dolls a few feet in front of me. Agnes took out her small personal pipe, lit it, and began to smoke.

Ruby moved off to my left a few yards distant and sat down on the sand. She started to beat her round single-faced drum in a gentle heartbeat. We were surrounded by darkness. Large night shadows that were still before began to encroach ominously on our circle as the smoke puffed from the pipe and began to billow out into the air. The smoke seemed to animate the shadows, obscuring them momentarily from the firelight. Agnes removed the blanket from around her shoulders and fanned it over the fire. The smoke made gleaming ringlets that hovered in midair and then moved into the medicine circle in spiraling swirls. She began puffing on her pipe and blowing the smoke directly across my line of vision. The air became thicker and more dense with a wispy gray pall. The smoke seemed unusual because it did not disperse in an ordinary way. I sensed the wind and thought maybe that was the reason. It became uncannily still. The light changed. The shadows on the smoothed ground appeared to filigree into delicate patterns, not unlike snowflakes.

The moon came out from behind high clouds and threw an eerie glow down among us. The brighter edges of the smoke were becoming luminescent cutouts in the brilliant glow from the moon. I was so transfixed by the smoke that I scarcely realized that I had never heard a drumbeat with such an extraordinary cadence. It was uneven, strong, and frightening. I looked over toward Ruby and could not see her. She was behind a deep wall of smoke. For a moment I could see the flash of her hands striking the drum in the dim firelight. The drum looked like a moon fallen to the earth, glowing from an inner source. Then it was clouded over by a dark, scrambling grayness. I looked toward Agnes, but she had also disappeared in the smoke. The only things I could see were the ghost dolls, and they, too, were being enshrouded in gray-white puffs. I was fascinated, watching them slowly fade away. A chill came over me as I realized I alone was visible.

Quite suddenly the moon went behind more clouds, and we were plunged into a thick, pungent darkness. The fire crackled and glowed. Two red coals shone like the eyes of a dragon, and then even they dimmed. For several minutes nothing could be seen. The smoke had a sweet, unfamiliar odor. I coughed a couple of times.

"In your mind, Lynn, go to the smoke," Agnes said. "Become the smoke. Smoke is prayer. Your spirit will strengthen there. Dream."

My eyes were blinded and burning, and the strange drumbeat rang in my ears. Ruby began to chant. I went with the silver, curling smoke, and it seemed to lift me closer to the Great Spirit.

"Overcome your hesitancy and become strong. Fend off your doubts," Ruby said in between her chanted Cree words. "Chant with me, Lynn. Dream your sacred dream."

Ruby's voice seemed to zoom in and then recede, as if it were traveling across miles of space. I began chanting and looking down at the ground. Suddenly I had the feeling that I was being watched. My head snapped back, and my mouth opened in a silent scream. Standing high above me, plunging up out of the smoke, were the ghost dolls, much larger than any human presence. The bone-keeper doll had a wolflike appearance and turned to me, its mica mirrors flashing like amber-colored eyes. Another silent scream pushed up from my deepest being. I screamed and screamed but could not make a sound. I tried to scramble to my feet in the murky darkness. A tiny bar of light appeared on my right, and I saw Agnes's hand travel its length, reaching my shoulder and shoving me back down. My brain felt as if it were full of smoke and the shredded ends of my emotions.

Then I saw the palms of two crude hands. I realized they were not hands at all, but great talons. They reached through the boiling smoke toward me. Pinpoints of brilliant light awakened through the mist. They were so bright, my eyes hurt. Slowly the lights parted. There was the bone-keeper doll, massive and alive. She had a strong, compelling face and proud, fierce eyes. Clad in feathery skins, her hair was pale. She stepped forward and back, forward and back.

Seeing this fantastically shaped creature caused a knot of pain in my stomach. I nearly fainted. Chill after chill ran through me. In spite of my icy terror, I was fascinated. The drum crescendoed into an unearthly, thundering roar.

The towering mourner doll danced forward. She had long, swinging arms and hair that was of a reddish-black color. Whereas the bone-keeper doll on my right had at first appeared frightening, she was in truth tender and kind. I sensed nothing of the sort from the mourner doll. She was violent and unhappy. She mocked the bone-keeper and, passing her eyes over my face, turned abruptly to face her. The mourner doll seemed overcome by rage and began to charge after the bone-keeper with a deathly grace. She swung her fists at the bone-keeper, who danced ethereally out of the reach of the blood-lusting swipes. Then their bodies locked in a battle for supremacy. The struggle was ferocious. The bone-keeper was able to hold her own against the angry, hostile mourner doll. It was difficult to discern where the turbulent smoke ended and the figures began.

"Watch carefully, Lynn," Agnes whispered in my ear. "You are seeing all that you are, your visible and invisible identities." For a moment, looking at the gigantic proportions of the creatures, I thought I would lose my self-control. Then Agnes whispered again, "But it's not enough to experience your true identity. If you think you are powerless, you cannot live. You will be locked in endless grappling and violence within the circle of self."

The reckless war continued to rage before me. My own inner awareness shifted to the wind, which was blowing out of the west. The smoke twisted in massive curls and spirals. The ghost dolls, who were entwined together in the smoke, began to spin back down to the earth. Soon the smoke cleared, and the dolls I had made lay quietly on their burlap beds. They had shrunken, and I was feeling just as dissolved. I placed my hand on the crude face of the bone-keeper, feeling the press of a fathomless darkness. I felt time running out all around me.

9

The Journey North

We broke camp after breakfast the next day. A breeze was blowing out of the southwest. The sky was cerulean and the cloud banks were thick and feathery. I was very quiet. Everyone left me alone, respecting my privacy. I took my pipe and medicine bundles down by the river. It seemed like a good place to be by myself.

It was a nice spot, with tall, leafy trees and the murmuring river sweeping by. I spread my medicine objects out on my red Navajo blanket. The grass smelled sweet and the birds were chirping loudly. I faced where the dawn had broken in the east and golden fingers of sunlight were tenuously feeling their way over the edge of the world. I thought about all of my recent experiences, those with Hawks-Above, Arion, and Twin Dreamers. I wondered if Twin Dreamers and Arion might be riding on one of those beams of light. I missed her and hoped I would see her again.

On the blanket among my medicine objects, I picked up the horseshoe she had given me. It seemed to belong with the ghost dolls. For some reason I wrapped it up with the bone-keeper in a red cotton cloth. Red is the representational color for woman and a good protection to hold the power of sacred objects. I always used red cloth made out of a natural fiber.

I knew that Agnes, Ruby, and July liked to be on the road early. I said a hasty prayer, put my medicine objects in order, and rolled everything up in the Navajo blanket. I went back to the truck just as Ruby and Agnes were finishing their tin cups of coffee. They both smiled at me.

"Did you say goodbye to the river, Lynn?" Agnes asked.

"I sure did. I'll miss her."

We had all been through a lot at this beautiful camp. July was off in the distance. Her arms were stretched high, and she was having a final discourse with the mountain. We left offerings of flowers, tobacco, sage, and sweetgrass to the spirits of place, then piled into the truck. I was looking back as we sped off down the road. From that perspective, it looked as though no humans had been there for a hundred years.

When I turned back around, I noticed that Agnes had been watching me. "You did a giveaway to the spirits of that land to break all ties with it," she said. "You gave tobacco and sweetgrass. It is good."

Ruby had an old moccasin in her lap, and she was re-threading the leather lacing. "Lynn always hates to leave anything behind," she said.

I shook my head. "It's true, I guess." I was sad to leave the camp where I had experienced so much, where I had seen so vividly the dichotomy of my temperament.

Agnes chided me. "You're standing in the swamp again, Lynn. You're addicted to feeling sad."

"You're right," I said. "I feel sad."

"Do you know why?" Ruby asked through clenched teeth. She bit the leather thread.

"Well, no."

"Do you remember the ice cubes floating on the waters of enlightenment?" Agnes asked.

"Yes, in the café. I do remember."

Agnes was gazing straight ahead at the snow-crowned mountains in front of us. They were blue-green, majestic, and sublime. "Ho," she said, lifting her hand to salute them. She turned to me. "Now, Lynn. Do you remember that I said that the process of waking up required very little? In fact, all you have to do is heat up."

"Okay, yes. I remember. It's a process of melting."

She laughed. "You began to heat up the other day."

"When was that?" I asked.

"When you lost the addiction of that primal sadness around your father, you conquered a magnificent enemy. Then your inward sun began to light up your medicine lodge. There was a lot of heat. Your body fires were leaping upward in flaming waves. That is why you traveled much further down toward the center of the sacred spiral. You nearly melted."

"Well, I hope she doesn't melt all over the truck," Ruby interrupted.

"I won't. I promise," I assured her.

"Don't be so sure," Agnes said. She spun another spiral in the dust on the dashboard with her index finger. "Look," she said. "You were out here, and now you've moved way down into this area." She pointed to two spots on the spiral's line, one on the outer rim and the other near the center.

"Does that mean I've gotten closer to my original nature?"

"Yes, much closer to the source. Or perhaps your original nature has come closer to the real you."

Ruby snorted. "Do you know what that means?"

"Not exactly," I answered.

"It means you're in a position more dangerous than being in a rattlesnake den. At the source there is no birth and no death. But if you fail, you may be scattered in fragments that will take you forever to put back together again. Either that, or the source will burn you up."

"It sounds sort of like Humpty-Dumpty," I said.

They looked at me curiously, and I recited the nursery rhyme for them.

"Yes, something like that," Ruby said. "You want to be cooked, but not eaten." She giggled and elbowed July, who was desperately trying to miss one huge pothole after another with her skidding front tires.

Clear of the bumps, the truck returned to normal speed and resumed its familiar hum.

"In a sense Ruby is right," Agnes said. She started to continue, but Ruby was quick to take offense.

"What do you mean, 'in a sense'?" Ruby blurted. "I'm always right. July, you tell them I'm right."

"You're right," July said, stiffening behind the wheel.

Agnes answered in Cree. An argument followed that lasted several minutes, both of the older women yelling at each other and talking at once. When they were through yelling, they both pouted for at least fifteen minutes.

"I'll continue with you, Lynn," Agnes finally said. "If a certain old witch will butt out."

"Gladly," Ruby said with a *humph*. "That's what I get for trying to be nice."

Full sunlight filled the cab of the truck as we angled off in a more northerly direction. I got my sunglasses out of my flight bag and put them on. Ruby adjusted the sun visor, and there were shadows over our eyes.

"The heat from that bright sun annoys me as much as Lynn does," Ruby said testily.

I made up my mind to try to ignore her for as long as possible. "Would you go on with what you were saying, Agnes?" I asked.

"Yes, I'll try," she said. "We were discussing melting. When you met the ghost dolls last night, you experienced the reality of your own individuality. You even saw your worthiness on earth, didn't you?"

"Yes, I felt my significance as a female warrior and my insignificance as another human, and the wonder or the miracle of existence."

Agnes looked off in the distance. She said almost absently, "We are in a mirage of life and death. What is gained is abundant, and what is lost is irretrievable and misplaced utterly."

"I don't think I'm equipped to talk about it," I said.

Agnes nodded to me. "I understand."

A red-and-white gas station loomed up in the distance. As we approached, I saw the old, rounded glass tanks. The sky was reflected in the plate-glass window, obscuring the oil-can display. We rolled in and squeaked to a stop in front of the regular gas pump. July cut the engine. We all rummaged through our pockets for Canadian bills and handed the money to July, who jumped out and began to pump the gasoline.

"You want a cream soda?" I asked.

Both Ruby and Agnes nodded. "Get one for July too," Ruby said.

I went in and broke a twenty. The sloe-eyed attendant barely looked up when he gave me change. He was heavy-set and cantankerous looking, with a gray handlebar mustache. He was watching an old, beat-up television set. I got the sodas from a machine and returned to the truck. July went in and paid for the gas as we all stretched before getting back into the cab.

I noticed that the attendant was following July. She got into the pickup and slammed the door harder than usual. The attendant stuck his head in the window and wiped his mouth with his sleeve. He leaned forward.

"We don't usually serve Indians around here," he said.

"We didn't order one," Ruby shot back.

"Only kidding, ma'am. You sure you don't want me to look under the hood of this thing . . . er, truck. Sounds like you got a barrel of wildcats in there." He slapped his leg and laughed at his own joke. His sweat-stained, crumpled, old Stetson nearly fell off his head. He straightened up and caught his hat, then shot tobacco juice through his gapped teeth at least ten feet. It struck me as odd that he did not have a normal belt buckle. He was wearing a thin clock instead in its place.

"Do you know what time it is?" I asked.

He looked down, then tried to lift up his stomach to see the clock, but to no avail. "Actually, this clock ran out a long time ago. It's late, I guess, too late." He pounded the hood of the truck and walked off in a dither.

"Oh, well," I said. "Now I'll never know what time it is."

"It's Indian time," Agnes corrected me. "That's when you do things when the time is right."

We all laughed. July pulled out onto the road again.

I was restless from being cooped up. I told Agnes I was perturbed by the ice-cube metaphor. I asked her to further explain melting. I told her I was having my doubts about my insights. I wondered if I had understood anything at all.

"Of course, you don't," Agnes said. "If you understood it, you would have melted. Lynn would be dead, and I wouldn't be talking to her anymore."

"Who would you be talking to?"

"No one," Agnes said, winking. "In Lynn's place would be a soaring eagle."

"I don't feel much like a soaring eagle," I said.

Agnes pointed to the dust spiral on the dash and then took a swig of cream soda. "Lynn, you were real warm. The ice cube was melting down, and that feeling scared you, didn't it? Be honest."

Ruby burped loudly. She slurped several swallows of her soda and said in a gurgly voice, "Lynn's always scared. I think she's just plain scared of Indians."

Agnes tossed her empty bottle behind the seat. "What happens to all of us when we heat up and stop losing all that energy in negative output is that we panic. We search for another way to get stuck in the swamp. Do you see?"

"I think so."

"Your mind courted sadness this morning, and you didn't simply witness it and let it go. You wallowed in it like an old buffalo in the mud."

I recognized how I tricked myself every day into worrying. I had so many ingrained behaviors and so many habitual ways of losing precious heat. I thought it possible for the perpetual fires to go out and put liberation out of reach in one's lifetime. It seemed unfair. I started to ask Agnes more questions and then decided it was useless. I could go no further in penetrating the mysteries. The veils of *maya*, illusion, would not lift.

"Why are we so afraid of realizing ourselves?" July asked. She slowed the truck to let five white-faced Hereford cows mosey across the road.

"Because we're like those cows," Agnes answered. "It's easier just to follow along in the herd, chewing our cuds and psychically asleep. We've come here to enter the sacred rounds, to be enlightened. You're not here to be a mother, a daughter, a writer. You're here to learn. I've told you this before, Lynn and July. We're the most afraid of the one thing we've come here to do. And that is to grow and become self-realized."

"But I'm not afraid of that," July said in a high voice.

"Then why aren't you realized?"

"Because I don't know much."

"Nonsense, July. That's another distraction, a distortion, a trick you've played on yourself. You don't have to know anything at all. You are already there, but you're terrified to see it. So the medicine process holds up one mirror after another until finally you look and you *see*. Each time either of you gets close to that central fire at the middle of the spiral, you feel like you're burning up. Just like Red Dog and his apprentices running out of that truck, you go looking for old familiar ground. In your case, old and negative habits bleed off that hot energy. I can use you two for stoves. If it gets cold outside all I have to do is hold my hands over you two, and I warm right up, because all your heat is leaving you."

We drove until the trees at the side of the road were black and the approaching night sky was gray. We stopped at a spring and made camp.

The next morning we were on the road again early. I was getting claustrophobic, the four of us huddled together on the truck seat. Agnes started checking the road behind us again. I wondered if Red Dog was stealing up on us. We drove until late in the night, then camped and resolved to reach our remote destination with one more long day's drive.

10

Thunder-Being Drum

It was late evening when we drove up behind Agnes's cabin. We had first stopped to let Ruby off at her place and then drove at once to Agnes's. The sun had just sunk down under the horizon, heralding nightfall with streaks of pink, orange, and crimson across the enormous sky. July and I carried in several cardboard boxes and various other things while Agnes was lighting her two lanterns.

"Oh, dear, July. Where are my blankets and my sleeping bag?" Agnes asked. "You didn't leave them at Ruby's, did you?"

"I'm sorry," July said, blushing. "I'm afraid I did. I forgot. I remember you telling me to bring them, but I guess I was tired from the trip."

"Well, I suppose I'll return with you and spend the night at Ruby's and come home first thing in the morning."

"Wait," I said. "I don't like to be here alone. Can't July drive you back tonight?"

"That's an inconvenience for her, Lynn. She's just driven two thousand miles. Don't worry. I won't leave you stranded. Just stay here and start putting the cabin in order. I'll see you in the morning."

Before I could say much else, July and Agnes left in a flurry. I waved as they got into the truck. I decided not to be afraid. In a sense I was glad to be left alone in the cabin, where my life had so drastically changed over the years. I had first seen Agnes standing here ten years ago. It was here that my teaching had begun. I placed my palms against the rough wall and felt around. The wood was uneven and splintery. The worn plank floors had swells, and the irregular window needed a cleaning. I was thirsty, so I made a cup of Postum on the gas stove and sat down at the wooden table, which had been moved to near the center of the room. I had felt deserted when Agnes left, but now was excited to be in the cabin.

I looked up at the rafters, which were hung with every conceivable Indigenous medicine item: herbs by the score, beaded bags, antlers, old rugs, fur in bunches, arrows, rattles, pipe bags, and shields. The sight was beautiful. I felt like the lost wanderer returned home after numerous adventures.

The feelings and sensations I was having made me think about when I had first met Agnes. So many years had passed. I had been an art dealer, and I had wanted to purchase a sacred basket from her. She had told me money would not buy the basket and that, in order to possess it, I would have to become her apprentice. Then the very idea had seemed absurd.

I laughed. Absently I picked up my spoon to stir my Postum. I became aware of a pulsating movement between my fingers. The spoon I was holding was swelling out like a snake and was radiating rainbow spikes of color. Then it started to curl around my finger. I shrieked at the top of my lungs, frantically throwing the spoon into the air. I knocked over two chairs and plunged headlong for the door.

I ran outside, bolted across the clearing in front of the cabin, then stopped. I was hysterical and gasping for air. My body was shaking, racked with tremors. I knelt down with one knee on the ground. I made a supreme effort to conquer my indescribable terror. After a while I felt better. I turned to face the cabin.

A woman appeared to be sitting on the porch steps, obscured by shadows. I stood, but my legs were shaking so uncontrollably, I did not move. Yes, I saw a woman. My eyes were not playing tricks on me. The light was pale and yellowish from the window. I tried to make a flanking movement to put the woman between the light and me, in order to see her better. I thought it might be Agnes or July, having returned to keep me company. I bent low.

"Agnes," I whispered.

There was no answer.

"Agnes," I called louder.

"No, I'm not Agnes." Her voice was familiar.

My teeth started chattering.

"Then who are you?"

"Twin Dreamers."

"I should have known," I said, approaching her slowly. She was leaning against a porch post, with her back against it, and sitting cross-legged on the planks. Her face was that of a female Methuselah. Her hair hung down in silver threads, tangled and thick, to her waist. Tears were running down my cheeks. "You frightened me so badly."

"I only meant to wake you up," Twin Dreamers said. Her face was broken with a crooked smile.

"You did that," I said. I was both laughing and crying.

I was so glad to see her. Now I did not mind that she had scared me half to death. I hesitated and then took her outstretched hand and sat down next to her on the porch. For several moments we watched the northern lights flicker in the sky, a pulsing rainbow of yellow, blue, and green.

"Arion is up there." Twin Dreamers pointed to the lights.

"Where?"

"All the northern lights are patterned on his belly. We are all made of the same light, but Arion has the power to show you."

"But I thought that was you in all those colors."

"It was."

"Then, I don't understand."

"There is no difference between you, me, and Arion."

"How do you mean?"

"We all carry rainbows in our bellies," Twin Dreamers said. "Let's call Arion and see if he'll join us."

Just then the sky filled with clouds, long, thin ones shredded by high wind. The aurora borealis was no longer visible. Twin Dreamers made a neighing sound.

Out of the darkness near the tall pines that were swaying in the southerly breeze came a soft whinny. A surge of excitement shot through my whole body. I stood up slowly to look. Walking out of the trees was a silvery horse. He was luminescent, like a ghost, and he walked out into a pool of moonlight. He tossed his head, reared, and pawed the air with his gleaming hooves. Sidestepping and dancing, as if to an inner tune, he slowly approached us, showing off his magnificent body from various angles.

Arion pranced up to me, cakewalking and tossing his head from side to side. His great, spirited eyes looked straight into mine. Then he gave a low whinny, nuzzled my face, and blew hot breath on my neck. It tickled and I giggled, blowing my own breath on his nose and rubbing his crested neck and deeply dished face. I had the most extraordinary urge to swing up onto his back.

"Go ahead," Twin Dreamers said, apparently reading my mind.

I thought about it for a moment, and then I grabbed two handfuls of mane and swung up.

"Easy," I said, stroking both sides of his neck. I whispered to him and caressed him. I felt his powerful muscles relax beneath me as he realized I was giving no commands and that I intended only to rest.

He nibbled some grass. I slid off, letting him graze, and went briefly into the cabin. I came back out with a cup of hot herb tea for Twin Dreamers and a package of Bull Durham tobacco. I set the steaming cup down beside her, took her left hand in mine, and gave her the tobacco. I watched her face attentively and said, with all the courage I could muster, "Twin Dreamers, teach me."

There was a protracted silence. Twin Dreamers lay the tobacco down on the gray planks of the porch. Her eyes showed amusement. She closed them and held my left arm just above the elbow. In the obscure light her face was a red-mud color beneath her dark brows. She seemed to go very deeply into thought. One minute her face was solid and opaque, and the next it appeared perfectly translucent. This odd perception was complicated by the way she would seem to reduce in size and then expand again. I attributed this to an illusory quality caused by the fading, shifting light.

She opened her eyes. They were like large, iridescent black buttons. "My way as shape-shifter can wake you up and help you explode your dream of what you suppose life to be."

"I think I know that, Twin Dreamers," I said after a moment.

"But there is no way you can actually know your dream, because you have not been there completely."

"Teach me," I reiterated.

"But you may not live. I don't know yet if you are a shape-shifter. I don't know if you can play with the sacred rounds of life and death and survive. I don't want to explode you."

"But you were right, Twin Dreamers. There is something deep within me that is obsessed with knowing your special path. I know you feel this desire in me."

"You have lived within your personal dreaming for your entire lifetime. You have forgotten your true nature, which existed before the dream."

"Yes," I said. "But I can learn, can't I? I'm willing to try."

"You have the best of intentions, but if the world as you know it should become elusive and disappear, and only you remained, you might not be able to bear it," Twin Dreamers said.

I could feel the wind stir. Her face changed expression within the shadows from the clouds. Her eyes were filled with compassion. "And what if all dreaming was gone for you?"

"I don't know," I answered. "I've never experienced that."

"There would no longer be a world for you, because all that you know, all that is Lynn and Lynn's world, is simply your dreaming."

"But I believe I have been aware of that many times."

"You have," Twin Dreamers said. She put her hand on the Bull Durham tobacco. "You are not really of this world. The world does not consist of this porch, the sky, Arion, and me." She patted her chest. "The world for you consists of your dreams."

"So, what you are saying is that we all live in our own dream world," I said.

"Yes, but what happens if I show you how to move your essence into another form? What good is that in your particular world? How can that help you?"

"I am not sure."

"Truly, the only wisdom to understand is that each mind is a world unto itself."

"Then if I no longer see the dream, I no longer see the world."

"That's right. So then, how do you live?"

"Do you mean how do I live without form?"

"Yes. You are accustomed to the false dream of form, duality and separation."

"Would I disappear?"

"Only if you chose to disappear." Those beautiful black, shining eyes of Twin Dreamers's met mine. "We in the sisterhood have been preparing you for many long years. You were not always aware of our presence, but many times we have been only a little ways off. You have become much stronger, so that now you are capable of seeing me. But perhaps I am a dream, and you are sleeping inside the cabin. Perhaps I am dreaming you. In actuality, both dreams are true. But what is crucial is for you not to be afraid when the twin dreams meet and touch."

"But I am. I must honestly say I am."

"You are standing at the edge of a great abyss. Your toes are curled over the edge of the Grand Canyon, and you are looking down thousands of feet." She paused. "Are you ready to jump?"

My words faltered. "I . . . I . . ."

"If you are, I will pick up this tobacco and accept it as your give-away." Her face was tender, but her whole body emanated an inner force that was indescribable. Arion nickered and threw up his head, as if to give me encouragement.

"Yes," I blurted out, wondering how I had managed to reply.

Twin Dreamers picked up the tobacco very slowly. I found it difficult to breathe and wondered what she would do next. She looked at me, and a crinkle began to play at the corners of her mouth.

"Two-time loser, huh? First you chose Agnes and now me." She kicked the sole of my shoe with her moccasin. We both began to giggle and then broke into a laugh. Arion, throwing up his head, looked at us and snorted the dust out of his nose.

Twin Dreamers reached behind her, toward the cabin wall. I had not noticed before that she had brought a huge single-faced drum. She showed it to me, holding it up to the moonlight.

I asked, "May I touch it?"

"Yes, but first remember who you are touching. You are fingering the spirit of horses like Arion and the many great warrior horses who have gone before him. Those spirits are delicate and lay themselves down to be called upon in ceremony. This drum in the wrong hands would be a terrible thing, not only for the person who stole it, for he would be trampled by a thousand ghost horses, but also the spirits could be injured and the drum might never be the same. Through this drum you can journey across time until there is no time." She handed me the drum with great care, and I took it accordingly.

There were many designs painted on the exterior, mostly of horses. Twin Dreamers ran her knobby fingers over the images and explained their mystical meanings to me. Then she said, "This is sacred. Never tell anyone what these symbols mean."

I said, "Thank you for sharing this with me, Twin Dreamers." This new knowledge had touched my heart and stirred it.

"The drum face is made from the skin of the greatest war-horse that I have ever known. He led many shamans out of the mists of ignorance and into the shaman lake. He carried many in the war against stupidity. His name was Thunder-Being. He gave away his life so that we could have this drum."

"Do you play it with that mallet?" I asked.

"Yes, this mallet is called his mare. It is his perfect counterpart. She plays him well and brings his being erect."

Twin Dreamers stood. Picking up a large wrapped and tied medicine bundle that had been sitting next to the drum, she motioned for me to follow her. Arion kicked up his heels and followed along a short distance behind us. We walked out through the stand of poplars near the cabin and journeyed an hour or so until we came upon a meadow shimmering in the moonlight. Twin Dreamers located a patch of bare ground that she seemed to like and squatted down. She smoothed out the topsoil with her hands and asked me to sit down across from her.

She began to sing in a guttural language I had never heard before. It sounded as old as time and was very haunting. At the end of her song Twin Dreamers said, "Here, unwrap this bundle. We must honor the spirits of this place."

She handed me a small bundle from within her own larger bundle. It was wrapped in rough red cotton and tied with two leather thongs. When I had unwrapped it, I laid it out and found a small candle, sage, copal, an abalone shell, a few yellow flowers, a small chocolate bar, matches, and a small pint bottle of Burgundy wine.

Not wanting to interrupt Twin Dreamers, I waited until her eyes met mine. I asked, "Now what do I do?"

"The spirits sleep in all the named and nameless things. They are fast asleep in everything. Yet there may not have been a ceremony here for the last thousand years. To us it seems like a long time, but it is but a breath in forever. The spirits of this power place wait and they slumber. When you, as a shaman, arrive, the first thing you must do is wake up the spirits and make them stand up. Remember that a ceremony is only as powerful as the person giving it. If you can't wake up the spirits of a place, you may as well pack it in and go back to your tipi."

"Tell me what to do, Twin Dreamers."

"Your bundle is open. That's right. Now light the candle. If it blows out in the wind, it is acceptable. Simply let the spirits see the light. Then light the copal and sage incense and put them in the abalone shell. The spirits love to smell something pleasing. This smoke will cause bad spirits to fly away from here. Lay out the flowers. Spirits love beauty. Then offer the chocolate. And next open the wine. Hold the wine in your mouth to mix it with saliva, for your own spirit, spray it out over the smoothed ground in the four directions. Then sing a chant. Call to the spirits to awaken."

"What kind of chant?"

"Like this." She chanted in a lovely clear voice:

> *"It will be as I say.*
> *Spirits, we greet you.*
> *We have the powers to bind it, cut it, change it.*
> *We have the medicine, the power.*
> *We have the light.*
> *We have the truth.*
> *We are medicine women.*
> *We conjure you to come forth."*

She stopped chanting.

"How do you know when the spirits stand up?" I asked.

"You may see their luminosity. We have called the good spirits, and they are beautiful. You may feel a slight pressure or a rustling touch. Now do with your bundle as I do with mine."

Twin Dreamers unwrapped another small bundle. She arranged the items in a select way, and I followed her, doing exactly as she did.

"Follow my song as best you can. Sing from your heart. The spirits want to hear your voice. They want to hear if you are true."

We sang, and I imitated the strange cadence of her chant as best I could. Somewhere coyotes were joining our song.

The fluttering candle framed us in cold, oscillating light. The incense smoke had grown thick. The mellow smell of copal and sage filled my lungs and enveloped us in a fine gray mist. Our song lasted for several minutes, until I began to experience the pressure or subtle presence of a hovering form near me. The manifestation was slight but very definite.

"Ho," Twin Dreamers said, ending the song.

She heaped a mound of earth and sprinkled corn pollen around it in a circle. Motioning for me to be quiet, she chanted another song for a long time. She drew the sign of the four directions in front of the mound and laid the horse drum on the central crossroads. She called it "Thunder-Being Drum" and drew two lightning flashes on the ground on either side of it with a staff from her bundle. Then she took three painted and feathered prayer sticks and stuck them into the mound. Each stick was different, and each one stood erect like a narrow chief wearing a headdress.

Sitting directly across the mound from me, Twin Dreamers wore an expression that was unfathomable in the flickering candlelight. She said, "Thunder-Being Drum asks you to pick a prayer stick. We do not know which path you walk. We want to speak your language."

I looked at the sticks and was immediately drawn to the one in the center. It seemed the least decorative of the three. It appeared stronger as well.

"The middle one," I said.

"Take it," she ordered.

I reached over and took it. The wood felt smooth and worn in my fingers. As I looked closer, I realized it was a drum mallet as well, with a hide bulb on the top above the feathers.

"It is good," she said. "The middle path is the path of the balanced warrioress. If you had taken either of the others, your power could have bled away in the delusion of obsession."

She sang a little longer in an almost trancelike murmur. Then she smudged the drum with sage and picked it up, holding it above her head. She looked like the goddess Isis holding up the moon. Picking up her mallet, she offered it to the Great Spirit. Following this, very slowly and deliberately, she began to play the drum. She held it in one hand, maneuvering it. The drum was at least three feet across. She was swinging her other arm up and down as the mallet reverberated on the taut drum face, sending a baritone beat out into the crisp night air. The spectacle was mesmerizing. She played as the Inuit peoples play their drums when calling the caribou.

I listened and was awed. The beat was instantly marvelous, enrapturing. I have always been ecstatic when I have had the privilege of being allowed to take part in an ancient ceremony whose roots are intertwined in primal and long-forgotten times.

First the drumbeat reached my heart. The feeling was strange and faintly pleasurable, like a smaller drum within my chest. I was not sure, but I thought I saw Twin Dreamers staring at my heart. My heart was vulnerable as she played. Our eyes met, and there was a dignity as well as authority in hers. The beat quickened with the flow of my blood, and the sensation moved downward. I began to feel the drumbeat in my solar plexus.

I heard Arion tramping around in the meadow, and then I saw his white, gleaming flank as he began to circle us. Twin Dreamers acknowledged him by beating almost the exact sound that his hooves made on the hard-packed ground mingled with the rhythm of her own primal beat. The effect was awesome, and I became lost in a cacophony of sound, rhythm, and the mystery of thousands of years of shamanistic tradition. A thrill hit me in waves, running the entire length of my body. I was more attracted to the tympanic depth of this drum sound than anything I had ever heard. I felt possessed by its beauty.

Twin Dreamers stood. The northern lights shimmered behind her. She began to reach her mallet up toward the blaze of the night sky. It was as if the aurora borealis were being pulled down out of the heavens by each of her powerful strokes, the light becoming part of her vibrating instrument. As I watched, my whole body was rigid from the ecstatic beauty of the spectacle. I saw and heard Twin Dreamers call down the northern lights and instill them into her drum. The round surface of the drum face began to glow with a subtle green-gold color. The edges of the drum began to fray and feather out into the blackness around us. We were momentarily engulfed in red, blue, and purple lightning flashes and sheets of pure orange light.

Suddenly Twin Dreamers was at my side. "Drum with me," she whispered to me.

I took my mallet and tried to trace her movements. It was as if some powerful, possessive spirit were using me as a rhythmic conduit. Beating the drum seemed like a part of my own being.

Twin Dreamers smiled at me. I caught the gleam of white teeth. "Continue. Drum like that." Her voice had retreated, and I realized she was calling to me, for she was already many yards distant. I was drumming alone, and it was proper. It was a ceaseless pounding that stretched out over all of creation.

I saw Arion rearing in the moonlight, and I heard his high-pitched rebuke. I saw Twin Dreamers running alongside Arion, stride for stride. I saw vast rainbows of color undulating up from his body, and Twin Dreamers had disappeared. But I heard her voice calling to me. "Lynn, leave the drum. Place it on the crossroads. Mount Arion and come with me."

Without hesitation, I did what this inner or outer voice commanded. I was not sure where the speech was coming from, nor did I care. I fairly flew to Arion's side and lifted easily up onto his bare back. We seemed bathed in an extraordinary shower of prismatic colors. Arion began to run like a meteor around the many acres of flat meadow. I lay down on his neck, feeling the power of the universe pounding between my legs. I did not become afraid until I had the sensation of becoming smaller. Or was it Arion becoming larger? There was a merging sensation. I looked down at my fingers entwined in Arion's rainbow-colored mane and saw pulsing rainbows emerging from my own hands. There was no delineation between me and the stallion, or anything else, for that matter. My consciousness imploded all at once. The curves of my body began to die, fading into the pulsations of the northern lights. I had the experience of being only golden light and becoming the golden shimmer of Arion's withers and neck.

Then I looked down at the ground, and we were at least one hundred stories high. I should never have done that.

"Don't look down," Twin Dreamers commanded. Her voice was within me. But it was too late, for I was terrified. I lost my concentration and my intent. I fell headlong off Arion's back. The last thing I remember was the cracking noise of breaking bones and a sound like a melon hitting bedrock.

11

The Chessboard of Forever

I was lost in the inexplicable dream.

It was almost impossible to find my way back to consciousness.
I kept getting lost down one glowing, ribbed tunnel after another. Then
I was in a wide room that had a gauzy, gossamer quality. I heard murmuring voices. Some spoke a language I recognized and some were so
far away, I could not really hear the words. A gentle wind blew over my
body. It was strangely restless and rode over me in fluttering touches.

I tried to move but in vain. I was one vast geography, and I could
not locate my anatomy in space. Then I inadvertently wiggled my
index finger. The shrouds of illusion that were ever clouding my vision
seemed to clear for a second. I had the impression I was lying on sheepskins, thick and woolly and soft under my fingertips. I thought I was
reviving, but I lapsed back into insensibility.

I heard trumpets and began going with the sound. I was gently
pulled forward and thrown backward with the melody. The trumpets
stopped. I saw a series of black and white horizontal lines. I was sucked
toward them. I was standing on a square of an infinite chessboard. The
color of the square was white. When I tried to leave it, I found it to be
quite impossible.

"Prepare to play the game, for the world of earthly delights and the
world of earthly sorrows." The words were spoken out of nowhere and
seemed to come from a voice that was both male and female.

Then I heard a definitely female voice say, "It's a game for any
well-educated lady. Don't miss it. It comes only once every thousand
years."

I heard some other giggly female voices.

"I'll play you for desirelessness."

"I'll play you for emptiness."

The male/female voice interrupted. "Stand by for the battle of the black and white magicians. The battle of the millennium."

I heard jabbering like a crowd of voices, whistles, and shouts. This turned into uproarious applause.

"How can you tell which ones are white and which ones are black?" a voice belonging to a woman asked. It was childlike. "Certainly not by their color."

"You complicate everything," another female voice scolded. "Look at the color of the square they are standing on. If it's white, they are white magicians. If it's black, they are black magicians. And if it's gray, they are out of the game."

"How very novel," the childlike voice said.

I looked down to see if my square were white, worrying that it might have changed to gray and I would be out of the game. But the square was still perfectly white, brightly so. I tried to say something, but when I opened my mouth, classical music came out instead of words. I tried to speak again, but this time it sounded like static on a blaring radio.

I noticed that my father was standing next to me, two squares away, carrying a sword. I tried to reach over, but my body was rigid, with no suppleness whatsoever. In fact, I could not move at all. I was frozen. Then I saw my Grandmother Bammie standing on the white square to my left. I wanted to hug her, but the same frozen condition prevailed.

"White king pawn to four," I heard the male/female voice call.

Then I heard a man's voice. It had a deep vibrato. It said, "Black king pawn to four."

I wanted to say, "Not very imaginative openings." However, when I opened my mouth, an old speech of John F. Kennedy's came out. Needless to say, I had not anticipated becoming President.

"King's knight to king's bishop three," the male/female voice called. There was a countermove by black.

"Queen's pawn to queen's fourth," the male/female voice said.

I felt myself moving, advancing ahead. It was as though I had dissolved and rematerialized two squares forward.

I wanted to say, "What would happen if I landed on a black square?" What came out instead was the sound of shattering glass. I shut my mouth in a hurry.

Moves and countermoves were called.

It was a very sophisticated game, in that the squares the people-pieces stood on would change colors. For instance, if a black magician piece would land on a white square, it would instantly change to black. Conversely, if a white piece landed on a black square, that square would instantly change to white.

I saw a man standing in front of me on a black square. I recognized him. He was a well-known philanthropist and humanitarian. I wanted to shout, "That's not possible. You couldn't possibly be a black magician." But what came out of my mouth sounded like an auctioneer speaking rapidly, taking large bids for a Picasso painting.

Another black magician chess piece was a famous politician noted for his liberal views. He had sponsored legislation to help the poor, and I had voted for him. I thought there must be some mistake. I tried to say so but to no avail. What came out was an old radio advertisement for a nasal decongestant spray.

Several more pieces were called and advanced.

"Black knight takes white bishop."

I saw the white bishop disappear off the board, and the black knight was now in my path. The part of the knight was assumed by an industrialist and financier I had once met at a party on Mulholland Drive in Los Angeles. I had enjoyed the man's droll humor. I tried to say hello, but my voice was an alto saxophone, which embarrassed me.

Still another black piece was a world-famous scientist who was honored for his work in particle beam physics. He was a rook. I could tell he was looking at me and wanted to wipe me out. The thought frightened me, and I wanted to say "Don't." What came out sounded like the noise from the track at the Indy 500.

A black pawn advanced by me. This piece was a woman. I knew she wanted to destroy me as well. She would have to get more power and maneuverability to do it. She wanted to advance to the white king's row and become a queen. Then she could have her way and take most of the white pieces off the board. She was a well-known entertainer who had dabbled in politics. Our eyes locked. For an instant her black square changed to gray, and then she vanished off the board.

"No gray pieces," I heard by way of explanation.

The game progressed with many pieces taken by both colors. I was amazed that I was still standing on the board at all. Then I realized that the pieces were as infinite as the board itself.

"Check on the white king by black castle," called a new, baritone voice.

The white king was in trouble and under severe attack. Much of the power of the black pieces was concentrated and being brought forward to attack the white sovereign.

"It's a stalemate," a voice called. "It can only be a stalemate. There are no checkmates in this game. There's no more chess for a thousand years. Time to put the board away."

The infinite chessboard quickly began to tilt. I fell, tumbling over and over. There was a light and a shattering noise. The light fractured into dappled kaleidoscopic patterns that fused back together again. The light had a texture. It had a thickness and pulled out in oblong limbs like those on a great oak tree. Each limb of light became a sculptured serpent. The snakes were adorned with plumed head feathers. They writhed like Medusa's hair. The sight became almost too bright to stand.

I finally began to open my eyes to see the light of day instead. I felt as if I were wrapped in a cocoon of cotton batting. The cocoon turned out to be made of many sheepskins. I was lying on piled-up blankets. I was naked. I rolled my head to one side. There were large crystals the size of ripe cantaloupes surrounding me. They were placed in a circle, and there must have been fifty or more. I realized I was in a large tipi. The light from the smoke flap beamed down in a circle that nearly matched the position of the crystals. I shut my eyes tightly, and then opened them quickly, trying to focus. The chattering I had heard became less remote and more understandable. They were strange female voices. Some were scolding. Some were soft and loving. Nearly all of them had accents.

I began to blink to clear away the film from my eyes, and for the first time the images became reasonably recognizable. It was like looking up from the bottom of a round fishbowl and seeing two dozen women gazing down at me. Everything was elongated and distorted. I felt nauseated. I tried to move, to sit up, and several brown hands gently pushed me back.

"Don't move," I heard Twin Dreamers say softly in my ear.

"Where is Arion?" I asked. My voice cracked in midsentence like a broken dish.

"He is outside," Twin Dreamers said. She held her face so close to mine that her long, scraggly hair brushed my cheeks. "Where else would he be?"

When Twin Dreamers moved back and joined the others, I saw a sea of faces. There were perhaps thirty women in the tipi. They smiled at me with great compassion and loving concern. I wondered who these women were. Then it dawned on me that I was surrounded by many members of the Sisterhood of the Shields. With this realization I started to cry. I was overcome. I was in the presence of illuminated souls.

I asked weakly, "What happened?"

"Fright," Twin Dreamers said gently. "And fear is a shape-shifter's biggest enemy. You must never run from fear. You must face it. Fear is a tracker that will hunt you down. He shoots his arrows just as you leap from one dream form into the other. That is what happened to you."

Ruby's face bent closer and came into focus.

"That's right, Lynn," she said. She patted my hand. "It's just like I told you. That fear of yours gets you every time. I don't know how you can be so innocent and contain so much fear." She held my hand and squeezed it.

"How do you feel?" asked someone with a familiar, heavily accented voice. She was a smallish woman standing at my feet. She was brightly dressed. I blinked and blinked. Suddenly I recognized her. There stood Zoila Guiterrez, the *curandera* that I had spent so much time with in the Yucatan. I had never understood what had happened to her. We were mysteriously separated. I had taken our relationship for granted, but then she had disappeared in a most disturbing way. My tears were flowing freely now.

"Oh, Zoila. It's you," I cried. "I have missed you so much." I started sobbing. I was so happy and astonished to see her. She placed her hands on my feet and began to massage them with care.

"Lynn," Agnes said. She had been standing behind me. "Stop weeping. Where do you hurt? We need to know."

I thought about it. Perhaps I was the locus of all the pain in the universe. Agnes placed her hand on my forehead. I let out a yowl of pain.

"Move your arms," Zoila commanded.

I did so very hesitantly because my whole body was shot with pain.

"I think my arms are movable," I said.

Zoila again commanded me, "Move your left leg."

At first I thought it was too painful to move, but with effort I lifted it.

I tried to stay alert instead of dozing. The many faces were still at the edge of my vision. The women of the sisterhood pressed in closer. They had a look of great intensity. This was magnified by the glinting, flashing crystals. With my tears my vision blurred once more, and I saw threads and tendrils of light attached to the women. I was so moved by the fact that they cared so much about what happened to me. I was ashamed of my mournful state.

"You're going to be all right," Agnes whispered in my right ear. "We, your sisters, are all here for you."

Zoila's voice broke through my tears. "Move your right leg."

I was able to do so. "It hurts the most," I said. "But I can move it fine."

Zoila eased up beside me and knelt down next to the mound of skins I was lying on. Her face was close to mine.

"I never thought I would see you again," I said, staring up into her piercing eyes, which reflected the shafts of sunlight like two polished obsidian blades.

"You can't shake me that easy, Lynn," she said with a big, flashing smile. "I'm going to check your body and see what needs to be healed."

She started removing several of the sheepskins from my stomach and chest. Then she closed her eyes. I heard a humming sound like that of an electric motor. It grew more intense and hurt my ears. I wondered if the women in the tipi were making the sound or if it were coming somehow from within my head. Zoila's hands were palms down, sweeping over my naked body about four inches above my skin. She began at my feet and then worked her way up the trunk of my body to my head. I winced.

"You're fine here," she said. "But you're very bruised."

Several hands rolled me over gently. I wanted to scream from the pain but had to pay attention to the event. Screaming would have taken too much effort. I was in so much anguish, I was choking and gasping for air. Zoila placed her thumb somewhere in the middle of my back and the pain instantly diminished. Then she checked my ribs, hips, and spine.

After scanning me, Zoila said, "You're all in one piece. But I think there is a problem with your head."

Zoila kept her thumb in the center of my back as I was rolled back over; then she slipped her hand out. This time it did not hurt at all.

"We all knew there was something wrong with Lynn's head," Ruby said, giggling.

I had to laugh. "Thanks," I said.

Zoila placed her hands on my head behind my ears. I yelled out loud.

"Sorry," Zoila apologized.

Running her hands through my hair, she gave my cranium a thorough examination. Various spots on the surface of my skull caused searing pain. Zoila was putting me through agony. She pulled the skin of my lids up and looked deeply into my eyes. "You have had a terrible blow to your head. Your brain rests in your cranial cavity in a kind of fluid. You have jarred your brain and bounced it around a little. Some of the time these traumatizing experiences can bestow extraordinary powers. Mostly not. In any case it is nothing to play around with. You've been exceptionally lucky. You hit your head hard, and that is why you were gone from us for so long."

I asked weakly, "How long was I gone?"

"Several days."

"I was?" That alarmed me.

Ruby blurted, "That's what saved your life."

"What did?" I asked. "I don't understand."

"Why, landing on your head, of course."

Everyone in the tipi laughed. Ruby had a distinctive giggle, and she elbowed Agnes.

I was feeling woozy and tired. I asked, "What happens now?"

"You rest," Zoila answered. "Let the crystals do their work. They know what to do. They're pretty smart. We don't think it's wise for you to be moved back to Agnes's cabin. Don't worry." She winked at me. "I think there are a few healers in our midst."

I wanted a long, long sleep—oblivion. I sunk back into the sheepskins, unable to keep my eyes open.

12

Cave of Mother Wisdom

The days seemed to collide into one another. I would wake up in the middle of a ceremony in progress. Or some nontalkative elderly woman would feed me some sort of bitter soup from a gourd bowl. Finally Zoila, who appeared to be my chief doctor, allowed me to roll out of the sheepskins and put my mended jeans and sweater back on. She and Agnes helped me hobble out into the meadow, where I could lie on a blanket in the warm sun near Arion. He came over and snuffled in my ear, then grazed right up next to the blanket. I closed my eyes and meditated to the even, rhythmic sound of him munching on grass. It was very pleasant, and I dozed off, then awakened with a start. Arion had come over, and, with his warm muzzle, made sure I was wakeful.

When I sat up, I saw that Twin Dreamers was sitting on my blanket. She must have been there for some time. She seemed intensely interested in me. Her deep eyes were tenaciously fixed on mine. I had learned in my short acquaintance with her that when she was silent, it meant she had something important to say. Everything about her seemed stark, from the faded blue cotton shirt she wore down to the tips of her moccasins. Red, yellow, and black glass beads gleamed from around her throat. The necklace was unusual in that it fit her neck closely, like a choker.

"Those beads are really different," I commented.

Twin Dreamers leaned closer so I could examine them.

"Touch them," she said. For an instant her eyes had a foxlike sparkle.

"So smooth," I said, feeling the worn edges of the rounded glass.

"They were a gift from a *cuna* shaman down near Panama."

"Oh, when were you down there?"

"Long time ago. Before you were born."

"Oh," I said, nodding.

Twin Dreamers tilted her head and looked at me. She was chewing on what appeared to be a piece of oshá root.

"You're better now," she said, still chewing.

"Yes, but it's so good to rest," I said.

More than a week had passed, and I had no motivation. The truth was that I was malingering. I had settled into an abnormal state of ennui. I fell back, stretching out on my blanket lazily and curling my toes into the grass.

"That *cuna* shaman told me that whenever I met a lazy girl, I should give these beads away to her. I promised to do that when she gave them to me, and so now I must keep my promise given so many years ago."

"Do you mean you're giving me the beautiful necklace you're wearing?" I asked. I was completely dumbfounded. "Because I'm . . . I'm lazy?"

Twin Dreamers ran her hands through her scraggly hair. She untied the sinew that held the beads and handed the string to me. Her eyes twinkled but her face was impassive. "These beads have very special powers from the southern jungles that could be useful to you right now."

She held it out and I reached for it. Just as my hand grasped the necklace, I heard a szz, not loud, but powerful enough to make me look. When I saw what I had in my hand, a great fear came over me. Staring back at me was a red, yellow, and black coral snake. Its tiny mouth was wide open. It twisted in my grip and tried to bite me. It was as if my body were hit with an electric shock. I screamed in fright, shot up from the blanket, ran backward, and threw the snake away from me all in one terrified burst of movement.

Twin Dreamers caught the writhing thing with her left hand. My eyes blurred for an instant. The red, yellow, and black necklace hung limply from her fingers. Her expression was enormously intense.

I stood several yards away, screeching at her. "Those coral snakes have nerve venom. They're deadly, always fatal. Why did you do that to me? I trusted you, and you tricked me." I was furious, shocked, and humiliated. My chest was heaving, and I was sort of jumping up and down, not knowing what else to do. Arion trotted over and butted my back with his head.

Twin Dreamers asked, "Why are you angry?"

"Because that damned necklace turned into a coral snake. It could have bitten me and killed me."

"Yes, it could have," she said. "But that was not the intent."

"What was the intent? Did you just want to scare me to death instead?"

"What are you talking about?"

"That snake." I pointed to the necklace.

"As you can plainly see, this is a necklace. It's made of glass beads, I believe."

"Yes, but a minute ago it was a coral snake. You can't tell me it wasn't."

"Was it?"

"You saw it too."

"No, I honestly did not."

"Twin Dreamers, I know you saw that thing turn into a coral snake."

"No. I am holding a necklace, but you are holding an idea."

"And just what idea is that?"

"The erroneous idea that these beads turned into a snake."

"Yes, I am."

"But that was only an idea. You thought you saw a coral snake."

"That's right. It was real to me."

"And you were frightened."

"That's an understatement. I was out of my mind with fear."

"Your fright was real."

"Of course, it was real. What do you think?"

"You are angry?"

"Yes."

"And your anger is a reality, but the coral snake was not. The snake was only a thought in your mind. You are needlessly frightened. You are escaping your fears. That is why you have been sleeping so much and why you can't get yourself going." She patted the blanket for me to rejoin her. I did not budge. Looking at the necklace, I still felt unsettled.

"Here," she said. She held the beads out to me. "I promise these are only beads. They're yours."

"I may be dumb, but not that dumb."

"Lynn, trust me. Your ideas are not your reality. There is something for you to learn here. Come." She said it so forcefully it sounded like an order. Very cautiously I stepped over and sat on the very edge of the blanket.

"Take this," she said. She held the necklace out to me. "Show me your courage."

I poked one black bead with my finger, then a red one. Twin Dreamers smiled. I traced a circle around a yellow one, and it remained a bead. Finally, I gingerly held the strand. The beads remained a red, yellow, and black necklace. I was relieved.

Twin Dreamers took me by the wrist. She examined my arm and hand carefully.

"I don't see any bite marks. Is it possible that you were bitten and don't know it?"

"No, I would know it."

"Then you were not hurt by the experience."

"Yes, I was. I was shocked and scared, and that was painful."

"But as you can obviously see, you are holding a simple necklace in your hands."

I looked at the necklace closely. I wondered what I had really seen. The snake had been absolutely real to me. But now I wondered if I had hallucinated the whole experience. Twin Dreamers was a powerful shaman, and she may have somehow transmitted the image of a coral snake to me. That seemed the most logical explanation.

"Listen to me, Lynn. When you looked down from the back of Arion, what did you see?"

"I saw the earth way below us, about one hundred stories."

"Now tell me, how did you feel?"

"I was terrified. I don't like heights."

"But when you looked down, you were safely riding on Arion's back. Is that right?"

"Yes."

"And what happened?"

"I was afraid I would fall."

"And then what?"

"Then I fell."

"So, what you feared the most happened. Is that right?"

"I suppose so, yes."

"Don't you see, Lynn. You fell because of an idea. The earth was not one hundred stories down. Look at Arion. He is a big horse. But not that big. You had the idea that you were up very high. But your ideas are not necessarily real."

"But, Twin Dreamers, that's what I saw."

"That's what you think you saw." She shook her head from side to side once and gave me an earnest look. "When you gave me the tobacco, I gave you a map, the only map there is to the seven spheres. I told you about your dream. I said when the world disappears, you may not be able to stand it. When you lose your idea of the world, you lose your world. So often we hold on to an idea so as not to lose our dream. And you literally fell for the idea. It could have killed you and almost did. It is that dangerous to the uninitiated, this world and this dream that you hold so dear to your heart."

"But you have to trust what you see."

"Yes, sometimes. But only if what you see is the Great Spirit. There is no world here where the sun rises and the sun sets. This light and shadow is actually the Great Spirit. There is only the Great Spirit."

Another week passed, and I was fully recuperated.

I discovered that the Sisterhood of the Shields was camped in a nearby meadow. A dozen or so tipis had been erected in a ring. I spent my days pleasantly visiting various members of the sisterhood. I heard things unknown to me, sampled delicious cooking, and hardly slept at night because of my excitement.

One night Twin Dreamers and I were out in a meadow. I was scratching Arion's withers and enjoying his company. As we turned to walk back to the tipis, two inky-black shadows appeared silhouetted against the moonlight. I was startled and hesitated, not recognizing who was there. Then I realized the forms were Ruby and Agnes. Agnes came forward.

"Come. We haven't much time," Agnes declared. "The stars have formed the pattern. The moon comes at last near the sign of the broken back."

As was usual, I had absolutely no idea what Agnes was talking about. I shivered. I wrapped my shawl tighter around my shoulders against a bluster of cold wind. We crossed the meadow to the other side. I was last in line, following behind Agnes, Ruby, and Twin Dreamers. The tree leaves were rustling in the wind, which was making a low howl. I heard Arion's whinny from behind me. He probably did not like being left alone, no matter what the reason.

As we walked through our small village of tipis, I realized it was deserted. The embers in the campfires had nearly died. An owl hooted ominously from the black branches of a tree. I saw a striped squirrel run across the ground in front of us and leap to a tree in a mighty jump. I was curious where we were going. I moved up in line to catch Agnes's attention. I was about to pull on her sleeve and question her when I heard the staccato sound of galloping hoofbeats. I whirled around.

Ruby was behind me, but Twin Dreamers was gone. I caught a quick glimpse of Arion running past us. His mane and tail were flowing like white water in a turbulent river.

Ruby moved up, and now she and Agnes walked silently, one on each side of me. The trees threw a network of moon shadows. I was becoming fatigued from the quick, stringent pace. We came to a flat, richly grassed area that I vaguely recognized. I had participated in a ceremony there years before.

"Be careful," Agnes said to me.

We began to climb down into a deep crevice that ran for several miles and widened into a basin. It may have been a dried-up riverbed. We slipped and picked our way slowly. The high poplar trees mingled their swaying branches in a feathery arch overhead, painting great swatches of light and darkness under our feet.

I heard a droning sound in the distance. At first it sounded like the howling wind. Then, as we walked around some jutting boulders, we looked down the long narrow valley lying dark blue before us in the moonlight. Shadows so deep they were almost purple appeared etched into the rock walls. The droning sound began to change to a higher tone, as if giant bees were hovering over pollen. I saw Arion on a ledge below us, rearing back. He was splashed with blue light and seemed like a sentinel carved from ivory. My blood began to rush and pulse at my temples. The whole night was dense with a vital force. My curiosity was extreme.

Then I saw the women. The Sisterhood of the Shields stood etched in deep violet against the weathered cliffs. They stood here and there, on lips of rock and on shelflike overhangs. The sisters were as a collective whole. Their skirts were billowing in unison from the dark wind. Arion stood above them like a regal crown.

Ruby and Agnes led me to an open position within the sisterhood. I took my place proudly. Like a fused watercolor, our dark blue shadows flowed together. Agnes whispered a word in my ear. It was a verb. She indicated with a nod that I was to join the toning or humming.

The sound was coming from all directions. The word was repeated fast in a clipped manner and produced the most uncanny, bug-like sound, vast and shrill, that was offensive to me. But the instant I joined them, I was no longer separate from them or anything in the universe. I was instantly swept along in the frenzy.

Agnes stepped forward and began to play her Elk Drum in fast, rigorous beats.

"Whatever you do," Ruby whispered in my ear, "don't move."

I had no intention of moving. I could not have moved had I wanted to. I felt as if a willow tree were inside me, rooted solidly into the earth and with branches caressed by the wind. The ground suddenly began to shiver under my feet. I struggled not to fall, because my first impulse was to throw myself to the ground. The cliffs in front of us were beginning to crumble. I had barely regained my balance when huge boulders and tons of shale tumbled from the top of the canyon. My heart was beating wildly, from anticipation and fear. As quickly as the drone of falling rock had begun, it was over. The dust settled, and we stopped our intonations. Agnes put away her small drum in her medicine bundle. I was not prepared for what I saw. A great gaping hole had appeared in the side of the cliff, like a horizontal teardrop. It revealed a cave or cavern on the cliff face across from us. I tried to look at every aspect of the new opening. It beckoned, large and black.

We all went forward in a procession and entered. The character of the deep cavern made a vivid impression on me. It was remarkably well lit from some unknown source and was roughly four hundred feet in diameter. The left-hand corner appeared inaccessible. The whole interior was an upheaval of pink dust, stone spires, and jumbled rocks. It had various tiers and ledges. We had entered through the teardrop mouth, but there were two other openings directly across and much higher up from the teardrop entrance. These openings were shaped like eyes. Through them the starry night was visible.

Several sharp boulders looked like serrated teeth, and there were various fissures in the rock wall and ground. The ceiling was hundreds of feet high. Painted on the bluish-black surface of the walls were clusters of luminescent stars and constellations.

"This is the cave of the Mother Wisdom," Agnes whispered to me as I was looking upward. "Painted rock sky is above you."

I saw the source of the light as I looked down. A perfectly symmetrical shield with a round, elevated surface, a kind of gigantic egg-like object, sat roughly in the center of the cavern.

"That is Nine Shield," Agnes said in a low tone. "It is a hunter shield and rests at the source of the great mystery."

"But what is it?"

"It camps in the faraway and returns every nine years. The hunters are children from the pebbly river. Be silent."

I had never seen anything even remotely similar. It had the glowing sheen of glass. One moment the shield appeared silver, the next bright yellow-gold, and at still another moment it appeared to be transparent.

The floor was strewn with small rock fragments, and I found it difficult to walk. I was afraid I was going to turn my ankle and get a sprain. Instead of encircling the great shield as I thought we might do, we climbed the stone steps to a ledge above the shield. This was the largest ledge in the cavern. It provided a kind of platform or balcony on which to assemble.

"Agnes, please tell me what we are doing," I said as we were forming in a half-moon circle in various rows.

"Remember this," Agnes said. "Power is peace within. The sisterhood in its collective vision has attained this inward peace while here on this sacred Mother Earth. We women are the guardians and protectors of our species. But our fate is in the stars. We are made out of stars. And to stars we will one day return. We are waking up the shield. It is a great privilege and an awesome responsibility."

The glow in the cavern dimmed. The procession had now organized into several crescent-like rows. Agnes, Ruby, and I stood behind thirteen other women who stood at the nearest edge of the rock platform. The rest of the Sisterhood of the Shields was fanned out in a row to both sides of us and also behind us.

A drumming began again, from the left and from the right. A soft, clear toning emanated from the sisters in the front row. It rose in volume and touched the cavern walls, so that it sounded as if it were coming from directly above. Slowly the repeated word became louder and louder, an unearthly wave that moved inward as much as upward. I felt a tension rising up in me from my feet and legs and into my loins. I was becoming feverish, radiating a sort of primal energy.

I wondered if everyone was feeling this sensation. I turned slightly to look at Agnes out of the corner of my eye. But her rapt, almost fierce attention to the proceedings made me turn and face forward. The toning had a kind of liquidness, and I was swept away on a vibrating current that now emanated from my heart. I relaxed into the spectacle of my own interior wilderness. I was beginning to see lights and a fusion of glittering colors. I did not know if this color storm was inside or outside my mind. It did not matter.

The toning was furious. It appeared as though tiny red, blue, black, yellow, and green crystals were bursting like aerial flowers along the path the vibratory current took. I glimpsed the iridescent tiny lights as they went down my arms, legs, and body. I could see the prismatic colors as they burst in front of my eyes.

I felt a gradual release as if I had been suddenly perforated and my viscera were leaking out. I knew instinctively that the poisons in my body were beginning to be expelled, the motion and vibration carrying them off in gentle jerks. I was so absorbed by these sensations that I paid no attention to what was going on in front of me.

Suddenly I felt a physical pressure from Agnes and Ruby, who were pushing and leaning against me. The toning stopped and I became alert. Ever so deliberately, the thirteen women who were in front of us turned, one at a time, to face us.

"Oh," I exclaimed as the first woman turned. She wasn't a woman at all, but a large, luminous grizzly bear. The animal stood perfectly still, staring across at us with a dangerous look. I squirmed from a deep shiver. I had to struggle with myself not to lose my courage.

Each of the twelve women turned and transformed into her animal spirit counterpart. Standing before me were the luminous forms of many creatures: A polar bear, erect on her hind legs, a deer, an antelope, a horse, an eagle, a wolf, a human-size badger, a red squirrel, a coyote, a mink, and a huge lynx tracking my eyes with hers.

In the center of these glowing forms was the largest creature of all, less luminous, but there was more light around her, if possible. She was a jaguar form of human proportions, and her face looked half jaguar and half monkey. Her eyes were large and round, her huge brows arched, and her nostrils flared. The ears were enlarged and jutting out like a monkey's. A coiled serpent held a tuft of Quetzalcoatl plumes atop her head. I thought she might be the jaguar-monkey goddess. She wore an apron quilted with obsidian blades pointing up and down, fitted together. I assumed it was quilted that way for blade combat. Buckled on her left arm was a jaguar shield and held upward in her right hand was a huge obsidian blade.

At first she seemed inanimate, yet I knew she had life. Then she snarled. Her jaguar mouth opened and she bared rows of pointed teeth and fangs. For an instant I thought I saw a tongue moving inside her mouth. Then I realized it was a human face staring out. I saw the shadow of a face briefly, and it startled me with its strangeness. She snarled again. Yes, something, a person, was inside!

Her unearthly quality unhinged me. I was frightened out of my wits, but also intrigued. A female voice from somewhere, perhaps the thing living inside the jaguar-monkey, said, "Name me. I am the central figure. Who am I? Name me and awaken the Nine Shield. If you have the power to walk out of your dream as a snake sheds a skin, name me. Then you will be one of us forever."

I knew instantly who the woman was.

I said, "The central figure is known by the name of Twin Dreamers." My voice sounded deep, as if it belonged to someone else.

I felt Agnes and Ruby relax next to me. The toning resumed and the sisters slowly turned back around to face forward. I did not know for certain that I had given the correct answer. When the women stood with their backs to me, I could no longer see their animal forms.

I had a sudden pain over my left eye that shot down from my eye socket through my neck, down my back and left leg. The ground began to tremble and the Nine Shield began to glow as if lightning were flashing from behind it or from within it. I wondered what the unknown substance was that composed the Nine Shield. There were oscillating flashes of cold blue light. I saw Arion. He was rearing up on a rock spur beyond the Nine Shield. He pawed the air, his ears flat against his head. He tossed his forelock and mane and danced from side to side. Arion was a magnificent expression of power and the pure rhythmic perfection of life. He was distant and untouchable.

Then the inexplicable happened. I am not sure how. But the gleaming Nine Shield lifted off the floor of the cave, rising twenty or thirty feet high, obscuring Arion from view. I began to take leave of my senses. The pain stabbing down from my left eye was intense and temporarily blinding.

"You are a daughter of light," Agnes whispered in my ear.

"Let go of your darkness," Ruby whispered in my other ear.

I watched the Nine Shield, and the light thickened. My eye caught explosions of red, blue, green, and fuchsia. The low vibration was becoming concentrated. It was as though we were all becoming pillars of light, throbbing and thrusting our energy out toward the golden Nine Shield.

The Nine Shield twisted in the air and shot out of the horizontal teardrop opening of the cavern. It hovered momentarily outside, then we saw an intense white light and heard an explosive sound, more like an implosion than an explosion. The Nine Shield vanished. The interior of the cave was utterly silent and dark.

The fires inside the ring of tipis threw curved and elongated shadows. I ducked in through the womblike entrance of one. The late-night air was cold. I made myself comfortable in front of the crackling fire. Plumes of smoke lifted up and flew out the butterfly opening at the top of the lodge poles. Agnes and Twin Dreamers were on my right. Our faces looked flushed and sunburned. I was exhausted, yet exhilarated from the experience in the cave of Mother Wisdom. I looked back and forth from one medicine woman to another. Agnes averted her eyes.

"I'm going to sleep," Agnes said. She gestured with her eyes toward her bedroll.

I took her hand just as she was rising. "Not until someone tells me what happened to Arion and what kind of shield Nine Shield is."

"No, Lynn," Agnes said. "Arion is in the mother hands. And I am very tired and need my dreams to revive me."

"That's not much of an answer, Agnes," I said.

"It must pass," Agnes said.

Agnes rolled up in her two old chief's blankets. Her salt-and-pepper hair extended out from underneath the edge. Her breath was heavy and the bundle she made expanded and contracted with each respiration. Twin Dreamers moved closer to me. She put her hand on mine and shook her head.

"Come," she said. "We might wake up Agnes if we talk here. Let's go outside and let her sleep in peace."

I ducked my head and followed her outside. We strolled up an inclined trail, not saying anything. When we reached a grove of maple trees, we sat on the soft grass. It grew darker as clouds obscured the moon. A nightingale was singing somewhere off in the hills. The only other sounds were the wind and the faraway moan of a wolf.

I apologized to Twin Dreamers for my impudence.

"We go into the soil blindly. Often what germinates us is beyond our intelligence. From the smallest seed rises the mightiest tree."

Tears came to my eyes. "I can't help it," I said. "So much has happened. Where is Arion? I miss him."

Twin Dreamers was seated cross-legged in front of me. She put her hands on my shoulders and looked at me for a long time. "Dry your tears," she said. "Arion is safe. He is part of worlds impossible to describe. Dreaming spans the worlds. Lay your head in the west each night and lead your life among simple things. You will meet Arion in the heart below the feathered bonnet of illumination."

"Do you mean dreaming?"

"Yes, return to your true self, where there are no separations." She raised her arm and pointed upward. "Before you is the universe. Remember that all things are sacred."

"What world is this?" I asked, pointing to the ground.

"You live in the world of the painted skull. But you are nearly ready to cross the barriers."

"The painted skull?"

"These things and what you think you experienced tonight are best not spoken of. There is no reason to unnecessarily lose the energy gained. We are here to learn. We all return to the dream. It is useless to try to discuss it. What is has the quality of that which is. As you are and I am, that is all."

Standing up, Twin Dreamers cupped her hands on the top of my head. Leaning down, she blew once gently. She held my chin in her hand briefly, looking into my eyes. She smiled slowly in that crooked way of hers. I could not help but laugh.

13

The Mating of Power

Night was coming on, and I could see a sliver of moon over the boughs of the trees. A campfire was blazing. There were six of us: Agnes, Ruby, July, Zoila, Twin Dreamers, and myself. We were out on the flat ground near Agnes's cabin. We had just finished a meal of salmon and roasted potatoes. We were drinking herb tea out of gourd cups. We had returned from the tipi encampment earlier in the day. July was chattering away, telling us how much she had missed us and how worried she had been since we had been gone so long.

"You seem well enough now, Lynn," July said. "You'll have to be more careful. The last time I fell off a horse was when I was twelve." July seemed to enjoy dwelling on my mishap. I was tired of her jibes and wanted to change the subject.

"How is José?" I asked Zoila. José is Zoila's husband and a wonderful man, a noted *curandero* from the Yucatan.

"José is fine. He has taken his apprentices down to a big ceremony in Xibalba in the heart of the mountains of Guatemala." Zoila's face warmed as she thought of her husband. I had spent a lot of time with the both of them over the past few years in the Yucatan, where I had basked warmly in the charm of their relationship.

"Your marriage with José has been an inspiration to me, Zoila."

"Thank you," Zoila said. "It has been an inspiration in my own life."

I watched the faces of the four elder women, all of whom were so important to me. They were so different and individualistic in their ways. Each had held up such vastly differing mirrors for me as teachers.

Of course, July was an apprentice like myself. But Agnes, Ruby, Zoila, and Twin Dreamers had one thing in common: They had all looked at the horizon line of their respective lives and had seen that it appeared flat. Each in her own way had made a choice, irrespective of what they believed to be right and true. Each recognized the fact that if she saw a destiny in her own path, the only way to fulfill that destiny was to simply do it. As Ruby had so often said to me, "You either do it or you don't. Don't mealymouth around about why nobody understands your purpose in life. You're just holding up the wrong pictures. Change the pictures if you have to."

Now that I had become personally acquainted with several women in the Sisterhood of the Shields, I realized that each of them had obstacles to overcome and struggles to endure. Each one had lifted herself off the flat horizon line of her life to a high plateau, where she could see the curve on the horizon. And in seeing that, she could know that everything comes around full circle.

"Be sure and say hello to José, Zoila," I said. "And tell him what I said about what an inspiration you have both been."

"I'll be glad to tell him, Lynn. But could you be a bit more specific?" She smiled warmly at me over the campfire. She noticed that I had gone very far away in my memory. I was remembering Zoila and José together. Her black eyes brought me back to the present.

"Not many shamans and people of power have strong monogamous marriages," I said.

It was a flat, dogmatic statement. Zoila toyed with the end of her long braid and considered it.

"There are many ways to live and many alternatives to marriage. But a solid and committed relationship is truly important to a *curandera*. Some people don't think so. But I do."

"Why is that, Zoila?"

"We are all female warriors fighting the war against ignorance." She indicated all of us with her chin. "We are trying to reinitiate balance onto the great *madre*." She placed her palms down on the earth.

"So how do we do that?" Her gaze rested on me, and I thought I had better answer.

I said, "By bringing the male and female energies back into balance."

Ruby snorted. "They never were in balance." Her face was like a dried leather rattle in the wavering firelight. "What do you mean, balance?"

Zoila went on speaking, ignoring Ruby. "We have to take our power as women. That doesn't mean become less female. It means to take our place as the goddess, as Xochiquetzal."

Ruby snorted again. "I never heard of her."

"Xochiquetzal is the goddess of change," Zoila said. "She is the mother of us all. She is like your White Buffalo Woman. We women must be that in whatever aspect. Then we can teach our men how to live. Otherwise, all is lost."

Zoila continued to ignore Ruby, who was quick to take offense. "That's right," she said in a high voice. "All is lost." She looked as though she were chewing a morsel from one of the long salmon bones.

"I think you are correct, Zoila," Agnes said. She was whittling on a piece of cottonwood root. "It is hard, very hard indeed, to maintain balance in a patriarchal world as a woman. If you can truly marry, then you can be a living example to your sisters and the society you live in. I mean not just a marriage fixated on the body, but a true marriage of the soul, where true intimacy is born. Balance begins in your own circle. Your life is then an art, and that is the best position from which to teach."

Zoila turned to me and smiled with great dignity. "Lynn, I would like to show you what you call a medicine wheel. I call it a completion sign, or a boundary-of-self measure. This might help you understand what I am really getting at. As you know, I am a healer in the old Quiche Maya tradition. I like to use other symbols that I have been taught by my friends in the sisterhood. The tragedy of all of our lives is separation. And I, for one, like to walk a bridge from my world to yours. With Agnes's permission, I would like to show you my interpretation of a wheel she taught me long ago."

Zoila turned with respect to Agnes, who was silent but nodded as she kept piling up slivers of cottonwood root at her feet.

"Yak, yak, yak," Ruby interrupted rudely, overturning several of our bundles like a bear in search of scraps. "How about some more food? I'm still hungry. Did anyone save me an extra baked potato?"

"Here, Ruby," I said. "Take my salmon. I've barely touched it." I handed her a partially eaten piece of the pink fish, hoping she would be quiet.

"Hmph" was all she said. She grabbed the fish and took a voracious bite, chewing loudly.

Zoila's face was blurry behind the flames of the campfire. She stood and came around to the right. She was carrying her staff, which was carved with symbols of the different spheres of existence around the circumference of the wood. I believed that staff to have mysterious powers, but I had no idea what these forces were. With the point of the staff, she sketched a foot-wide medicine wheel in the earth. She sat down and put a black flat stone at the west side of the circle.

She said, "On this wheel, emotion lives in the west, here where I have put the stone. That is where women live predominantly, in their emotions. In most traditions emotions reside in the west."

Twin Dreamers lay down on her stomach, propping her head up with her hands, which looked like old, twisted boughs. Her hair nearly covered her face, and her legs bent at the knees. She dangled her moccasined feet over her back, so that she looked like an ancient child listening with rapt attention to a fairy tale.

Zoila went on, positioning herself to the east of the wheel; I sat in the south. Agnes was off to my right and Twin Dreamers was in the west. July and Ruby watched none too respectfully from a few feet away.

"In the east is mind," Zoila said, placing a striped rock on the wheel. "Men live mostly in the mind, in the east. Find me another stone, Lynn, and put it in the south."

I searched around on the ground and found a reddish-brown, five-sided rock. I placed it on the wheel in the south.

As soon as this was done, Zoila said, "The south is substance, the physical."

Twin Dreamers smiled and held up a white, shiny stone in her left hand. She gave it to Zoila.

"Perfect," Zoila said, examining it. She placed the white stone in the north. She said, "The north is intuition and spirit." Using her staff, she pointed to the top of the circle near the white rock. Then she indicated the west and east positions and drew two lines meeting in the south. She had drawn a V, or an inverted pyramid. She said, "Men and women in relationships meet in the south for physical encounters. Then they return to the east and west, and they talk about what they feel. And then they talk about what they think.

"Lynn, you have said that José and I are an inspiration to you, so I will use us as an example. Also, you know us. That kind of example you can grasp. José and I met in the south to make love. Our love was so inspired and so great that our instincts were reawakened. We shot up to the north, into intuition and spirit. It is our instinctual nature that drives us up into the north. As you may be able to see, most relationships don't have any north. Their interaction is all east, west, and south. The unfortunate thing is that often two people make love and awaken their instincts for the first time since they were three years old. The re-introduction of spirit into their lives is so overwhelming that they think they are in love, and they marry. But then the cruel edge of reality cuts them to ribbons. The reason is this." Zoila etched another line, straight across between east and west. She continued. "You see, they are thrown back into east-west life experiences, which consist of who brings home the bacon, who takes out the garbage, who pays the bills, and so on. Then there is the endless discussion of what I think about what you said and what you feel about what I think. And occasionally they make love to have babies. So what is left out after they become familiar with each other?"

I said, "The north."

"That's right," Zoila said. "And that's what I think your psychology doctors lose sight of. They immerse a person in an endless east-west discussion. This is what you feel, and this is what I think, and so on. I have worked with many people who spent years with the psychology doctors and were never healed. The movement in any relationship between the east and west promotes understanding and knowledge. But enlightenment and intuition and spirit come from a south-north movement, one that is motivated by your instincts. If you live without the north-south, you feel as if you are losing your soul. You feel like you are dying. There is transformation in movement between north and south, but never between east and west. That is why so many men and women go out on their mates. They feel like they are losing their souls, and they don't know why. If you live an east-west life, you are living only a part of your totality. You are not living the full wheel, and part of it simply atrophies."

"I can understand the model, Zoila," I said. "But how do you maintain a north-south relationship?"

"First of all, you take power as a woman. Then you will attract a man who has taken his power. That is the beginning. Nothing meaningful can happen until you stand in the center of your own wheel. Then you re-establish your instinctual nature, the attributes society has denied you. That means sexuality, survival, and so forth, the needs of your intuition and spirit. You merge your soul with another's soul through creativity with another human being."

"Do you mean that you work together?" I asked.

"Yes, in some important way."

"Then how do people who have diverse careers get together?" I wanted to know.

Zoila leaned back on her blanket for a contemplative moment. The fire made a peculiar cracking noise, leaping up to intensify her dark Maya face. She said, "It's difficult. Men and women have to learn to be creative together. In your society, the man could work in insurance and the woman work as a nurse. But they could find each other in a mutual study of shamanism, for instance, or in a shared love of poetry. Men and women need to find something that involves the manifestation of spirit into substance and substance back into spirit."

"How about writing?" I asked.

"Yes. Writing could be very good. You bring an idea in the form of spirit and intuition down from the north and manifest it in a physical book. You write physically. It reaches out to people on an intuitional level, and you receive substance—that is to say, money—in payment."

Twin Dreamers rolled to one side and surveyed me. "Lynn, do you remember when I spoke to you about the mountain lion coming down and becoming a sheep?"

"Yes."

"I was speaking, as you remember, about your instinctual nature. That was symbolized by the mountain lion. You cannot be a spirit warrior without a strong relationship with your instincts. That inborn wildness moves you north and south on the wheel." She reeled back, holding her chin in her hands and crossing her legs above her back. "When you see a shamaness, you realize there is a potent force around her. You wonder at the manner of this force. It is strange, indefinable. This woman of power is going against the grain of the wood. She is swimming upstream against the current. That creates a very unusual and powerful energy of its own kind. A female warrior knows how to use that energy. By being a woman in this male-oriented life, she is changing the direction of the current, just by being a woman in this position. When enough women swim against the current, it will change the current forever. Then if she becomes a warrior, she has double the power and twice the energy. Once she knows how to use it to her advantage, she knows how to live with danger. She is dangerous herself. She is living with vision among people who have eyes but cannot see. They will want to blind her and take away her vision. She is preserving a tradition that is ancient, sacred, and unknown to most."

"Well put," Agnes said.

"The female warrior knows that life is an adventure of the spirit," Twin Dreamers went on. "She knows that this earthwalk is only a dream born of a greater dream beyond our imagination."

She leaned forward toward me, her round face and scraggly hair hovering over the circle Zoila had drawn. We all observed her. Her movements were so strangely awkward that she was mesmerizing to watch.

Zoila pointed to the circle with her staff. She pressed and made a mark with it. "That is another reason why it is profound and difficult for power people to find each other and mate."

"What do you mean?" I asked.

"The pride of a shamaness is different from ordinary pride. It is a pride born of inner truth. It is not an ambitious pride concerned with outward accomplishment. It is a pride of knowing, of *seeing*. It is a pride of sorrow for the blindness that everywhere surrounds her. One moment of vision is worth an eternity of darkness. A shamaness is so used to going upstream, she has most likely always felt alone. It is hard for her to stop long enough to recognize someone and to let them into her circle. That is why the lesson of trust is so prominent in the lives of most *curanderos*, male or female. That lesson is the trust a female warrior must place in her instincts, the wildness of her own soul that she will never allow to be tamed."

Agnes sat forward. She pointed to the east and west on the circle, sweeping her hand back and forth. "We lose our wildness and become tame when we consistently move east and west on the great wheel. We are mountain lions becoming sheep, pretending to be creatures we are not. And we wonder why there are rapes, murders, and wars. We become violent in our tameness. The gateway here is instinct because it makes us move. There is no enlightenment without movement south and north on the medicine wheel. And that is how a fruitful relationship comes into being." She stood up.

Ruby came over and nudged her. "I like one-night stands better," she said.

We all laughed at Ruby's antics. She was acting like a vamp, a bar-room floozie. She ran her hands suggestively down along the sides of her body, exaggerating the curves.

"Come on, July," Ruby said, taking her by the hand. "Let's go into town and find us a hunk."

July smiled and rose.

"Good-night, girls," Ruby said. "July and I are going to beat the bushes and see what we can scare up."

We all said good-night and hugged Ruby and July. The two of them took off down the path leading to Ruby's cabin. Ruby was swinging her hips outrageously, and we all laughed at her again until she disappeared into the darkness.

Agnes rolled up her blanket and threw it over her shoulder. She said, "Ho. This is one medicine woman who is going to bed. I will send you all good dreams."

We all hugged Agnes and watched her walk to the cabin.

Twin Dreamers, Zoila, and I talked for an hour longer until the embers were dying in the campfire. The three of us decided to sleep in our blankets under the brilliant stars. I gave Twin Dreamers and Zoila big hugs and got comfortable in my bedroll. I thanked both of them for their good medicine talk. Zoila was already curled up and sleeping. These medicine women had shown me an aspect of my own character that I had desperately needed to understand. I was deeply grateful.

The wind came up, bending the long shoots of grass. I moved my bedroll closer to the fire and threw a log on the coals, hoping it would catch later. I began to think about Arion and how I had once slept in the curve of his beautiful neck. Tears came to my eyes as I thought about the great horse. I loved him so much. The stars lighted the sky in a glittering blanket, the pebbly river, as Agnes called it. I wondered if I would ever have the honor of seeing Arion again.

An owl began to hoot softly from the direction of the wind. I wondered if the night cry was an omen of good or ill.

14

The Secret of Mastery

Twin Dreamers came inside Agnes's cabin very early the next morning. I watched her; I had come in early and was writing. She paused in the entrance before coming in and closing the door behind her. The light was playing tricks and swept around her in pointing fingers. Her hair was still wet and dripping. She had evidently just washed it in the creek. She took a knife and cut the strands that straggled over her eyes. She threw the clippings in the stove.

It amused me that she looked at herself in an old smoky mirror and seemed pleased with her image. She was wearing green pants and an embroidered blouse from the Yucatan.

"You look pretty together for a thousand-year-old woman," I said in a kidding voice.

She turned, startled. Her black eyes twinkled with a darting flash of astonishment. "I thought you were still asleep, Lynn." She grinned. "Maybe we should wake up Agnes too."

"I'm sure she'll get up soon. It's not like Agnes to sleep late. Although, she has seemed tired lately."

Just then Agnes rolled over and sat on the side of her bed. "It sounds like a hog-calling contest in here. How can anyone get any sleep?"

Twin Dreamers and I both apologized for waking her.

In a few minutes we had breakfast on the table—biscuits, honey, and sage tea. We were all in a great mood. We were eating with relish when Ruby and July walked in. Agnes got up and gave them both a big hug. She motioned for them to sit down and put some more water for tea on the stove. Then she placed the biscuits in front of Ruby and July.

"Thanks, Agnes," July said, smiling. She dipped happily into the honey pot and left a long amber string on the wooden surface of the table.

"Where's the berries?" Ruby asked loudly. "I don't see them. Don't tell me you have no berries."

Agnes shrugged her shoulders. She said, "We're fresh out of berries. Perhaps if I had someone to pick them for me, I would have some berries."

All eyes turned away.

"I was just thinking about that," I said. "Twin Dreamers, why don't you and I go pick some berries for Agnes?"

"And Agnes's guests," Ruby quickly added.

Twin Dreamers looked fresh and particularly animated this morning. She fluffed out her freshly washed hair with her right hand. She looked at me and then at Ruby. "We'll go pick you some blackberries, Ruby," she said, smiling at her.

Ruby's demeanor changed. She reached into her Pendleton shirt pocket and brought out a tiny ivory horse figure. "Twin Dreamers, I want to give you a gift," she said. "I thought you might like to have this horse figure."

"Where on earth did you get that?" Agnes asked. "It's beautiful."

"Yes, it is," Ruby agreed. "I believe it has significant powers, but I have been unable to determine what they are. I found it lying on the ground in the cave of Mother Wisdom when we were leaving the ceremony. I almost turned an ankle when I stepped on it." Ruby turned the statuette in her hand. "I think it was meant for you, Twin Dreamers."

Twin Dreamers was impassive, but her deep-set eyes were filled with admiration. She opened her left palm to receive the horse. Her eyes misted over for a brief instant; then she held the horse figure up to the sunlight. In the beam it was somewhat translucent. All eyes were on it.

"Medicine dog," Twin Dreamers said. "That is the old way of saying *horse*." She handed the figure to me with a smile. "I wonder where it may have come from?"

On closer examination, I saw that it was carved and etched around the flanks. It was rearing and had a long white mane and tail. Everyone examined it and had comments to make. Finally, it was passed around to Twin Dreamers again. She said, "Ho," and put it in the pocket of her Guatemalan shirt.

Agnes thrust a large basket into my hands. "Here," she said.

"Where is the best place to pick them?" I asked.

"If you go down the path by Dead Man's Creek, beyond the first thick stand of trees, you'll find more blackberries than you can carry."

"My mouth is already watering," Ruby said.

"I can go too," July said.

"No, July." Agnes pushed her back down in her chair. "I have some medicine work for you to do for me."

July brightened. "What's that, Agnes?"

"Oh, sweep, dust, carry water, and chop wood." That deflated July.

"Okay, we're gone," I said, opening the door.

"Good berry picking," July said meekly.

With me carrying the basket, Twin Dreamers and I set off down the path to the creek. The sun was brilliantly reflected on the poplar leaves. I drank in the sound of the wind through the high branches and glanced up at the stark white cloud formation cascading above us in fast-moving air currents. We took a new way, a shortcut, to the upper waters of the creek. We found ourselves struggling around crowded crags of slate stone jutting out of the marshes. Eventually we came to the blackberry clumps and patches that were growing over fallen pine logs.

"Be careful of the stickers," Twin Dreamers admonished.

"That I will do," I replied.

I had not picked blackberries since I was a child, and I kept scratching my hands and arms as I reached through the brambles. So much for being careful.

Twin Dreamers saw my discomfort and laughed.

"I don't think it's very funny," I said.

"Mastery is the secret here," she said. "Watch how I place my fingers—this way." She demonstrated her superior powers of blackberry picking. She reached through the stickers without so much as a scratch. "You see, I come from a long line of berry pickers." Her lips twisted in that odd smile. "It's all in the lineage, you know. You have to be born to it." She was picking handfuls of berries while I could only manage to extricate one single berry from a branch at a time.

"What are you getting at?" I queried.

"Mastery is a teaching here."

"What do you mean?"

"I mean you must be willing to go to the bottom." Twin Dreamers was lying on her back under the bush and looking up at me through a maze of brambles.

"I see," I stated, struggling for another single berry with my scratched and bloody fingers.

"You have to be willing to have badger dung thrown at you for your mistakes. You have to be willing to beg, to stand on some street corner and sell your ability for nothing."

"What then?" I asked.

"Then, if you have the ability, people will find out that you are really accomplished, that you have learned mastery. They will sit down at your feet and listen to what you have to say."

"What is the purpose of mastery?" I asked in a garbled voice. I was sucking on one of my mutilated fingers.

"A lot of people want mastery for different reasons, so they can't be scratched or whatever. Perhaps they want money or a big airplane."

"But why you, Twin Dreamers? Why do you want mastery?"

She laughed. "I would say that I want mastery just to know if I can handle it."

"Well," I said, taking several berries at one pick. "I can say those are my motives too."

I was beginning to get the hang of picking blackberries. Certainly I was nowhere near as accomplished as Twin Dreamers, but I was a lot better than when I first began. I was beginning to fill one corner of the basket. The berries were nicely sized and ripe, and every so often I would pop one into my mouth. They were delicious. I saw that Twin Dreamers was eating a portion of her berries also.

"Sometimes you just have to be born to something. If you have the lineage of being the chief, the king, a medicine woman, anything, then you must draw your lance. And by that I mean you have to be willing to do whatever it takes to be the master of what you do."

"What do you mean by lineage?" I asked.

"I meant it as a twin sister. Lineage means courage. Do you have what it takes? When you get scratched time and time again by the thorny brambles, will you go home crying, or will you ultimately master the art of berry picking and enjoy the rewards? That's all." She picked the basket up off the ground. It was mounded over with berries, completely full. We both were pleased. "Let's go," she said.

As we were returning, I said, "You know, I read somewhere that if you can't stand before the mast, you shouldn't be sailing. Is that the lesson of the berry patch?"

She nodded and put a berry in my mouth.

15

The Shaman's Myth

The next afternoon I was sitting on Agnes's porch drinking a cup of tea when I saw Zoila approaching with two women. I recognized them as members of the Sisterhood of the Shields. They were the members closest to me in age. When the three of them saw me, they stopped in their tracks. I watched the two women say goodbye to Zoila and return in the direction from which they had come.

Zoila approached. I got up and we hugged, then I went inside and brought her a cup of tea. When we were settled comfortably, Zoila said, "You seem very interested in those women."

"Well, yes," I said. "But I wasn't going to be rude and ask a lot of questions."

"Those women are like you. They are full of eagerness and enthusiasm. They each hold a whip with which to flay open all the doorways. Like you, those women were seekers. They were once dabblers in everything. Wasn't that true about you, Lynn?"

"Yes, I suppose it was."

"Haven't you told me you studied yoga and Sufism, for example?"

"Yes, I have. And many other teachings."

She chuckled. "You make me laugh."

"Well, it's better than watching television."

Zoila shook her head. "Most of humanity tries to huddle in secure domains. Yet there are always those few we call walkers on the edge or rim. They are searching for a bridge that leads over the river. There are many bridges. Some of these are masked under the name of religion. Yoga is a bridge. Sufism is a bridge. In the end there is only one bridge to follow, and that is the bridge of love. That bridge is the singular way to span into the beyond. Ultimately that is the one that gets us all there. When you experience the unexpected and the unprecedented in your life, follow your heart. It's the one sure path that leads to safety."

We talked for a while. From inside the cabin, I could hear the clinking of dishes and Agnes giving instructions to July. The smell of pine smoke was thick in the air, rolling up in gray streamers from the chimney. We could also smell fowl and pastry baking.

Agnes came out and, with a wink, she said, "Dinner is on the table, ladies. You better come in before Ruby eats it all."

"Don't mind if we do," Zoila said happily.

We went inside and ate.

After dinner Twin Dreamers and Zoila and I sat on Agnes's porch. The northern lights splashed subtle shades of green, gold, and pink across the evening sky. The upper branches of the trees shuddered in the wind. Darkness was coming on.

Agnes and July had prepared a wonderful meal of quail, wild rice, and blackberry pie sweetened with honey. We had all eaten ravenously and now were relaxed and content. Agnes, Ruby, and July had walked down to the creek to repair the sweat lodge. Agnes had said that we would do a sweat ceremony later in the week. She wanted to make sure that everything was in order with the fire rocks and the wood supply.

A large mother raccoon marched in front of us, leading her four babies. The sight amused us all. Then a gray squirrel peeked over the porch boards a few feet away from Zoila. The squirrel's fur nearly matched the color of the gray planks. She shivered in excitement at her own courage. Then she scolded us with a flick of her tail. When I turned my head, she uttered a loud chattering sound and scurried away to her nest in one of the big pines.

Zoila moved closer to me on the porch step. She stared at me for a minute and then put her hand on my solar plexus. She closed her eyes.

"What?" I asked. "Is something wrong with me?"

"Apparently you are very well centered," Zoila finally said. "Now put your hand on the same place on me. Tell me your impressions."

I placed my hand on her solar plexus and held it perfectly still. I closed my eyes and went into my medicine place. I felt a strong flow of energy and said so.

"Now try with Twin Dreamers," Zoila said.

I scooted over to Twin Dreamers. I placed my hand on her solar plexus. The impression I got was curiously very different from the one I had received from Zoila. I did not know what to say. I felt a kind of emptiness or nothingness.

Zoila was watching me expectantly.

"It feels empty," I said.

This brought that odd smile to Twin Dreamers' face. She chuckled softly to herself. I took my hand away.

"It is empty for a reason. Twin Dreamers is a healer also. But she heals within the dream, the twin dreams—yours and hers. So to see and feel her energy you have to look out here."

Zoila ran her hand in a sweep several inches around the periphery of Twin Dreamers' body. She indicated with her hand the surrounding etheric energy field.

"Twin Dreamers' energy is very pronounced," Zoila said. "It is sensibly controlled and out here like a shadow. We are all three in the healing arts, shamans. But we work differently. Twin Dreamers works in the dream. I work with herbs and the physical body almost exclusively. I know the range of the plant spirits. And you, Lynn, heal the mind and the heart. That is why an idea can attach itself to you, and you can actually become afraid of a thought. For example, that is the way in which you became afraid of heights or falling off a horse."

"How does that follow?"

"Because we shamanize what we understand and have lived through. Your father taught you about fear, heartache, and mental chaos. You had to dig yourself out of a big hole that could have become your grave. You healed yourself as we did. You learned of your powers, so now you can heal others in the same way." Zoila took an apple out of her pocket, threw it several feet into the air, and caught it. She took a big bite, then offered me one.

I patted my stomach to show her it was full. She went on eating.

"I would like to leave you with a present, Lynn, an *idea*," Twin Dreamers said. Her eyes twinkled, and her scraggly hair was ruffling in the gentle breeze.

"What do you mean, *leave*?" I felt my insides clutch.

"The omens are promises, but only if you follow them. For instance, let's say that I would like to give you not only a present, but something to think about as well." She inched over closer on the porch steps. She held the little ivory horse figure in front of my eyes. It was the one Ruby had given her. "I see my history and my vision in a horse's eyes."

"Why this horse particularly?" I asked.

"Each shaman has a secret. All of her energy comes from her myth. My myth is the image of the horse, which to me is freedom."

"Freedom?"

"Yes, there is freedom in the sound of the hooves carrying me through space and time and other dimensions of reality. When I become the horse, I am created from thunder and lightning. I reclaim the horse. I participate in that plane of sympathetic magic. I am the apocalyptic energy of horse, of life and death. As a horse gallops, I, too, approach you as in the ceaseless movement of the ocean's waves." She used her hands to help express her words. She set the little ivory figure down in her lap. "To shamanize someone, you look at what they can become, not just what they appear to be. Look at the magnificence of possibility in an individual. And then look at what they are, and you locate their pain, their tragedies, their incompleteness. This creates a space between what is and what could be. It is in that void that enlightenment exists. It is from here that we all come and must again return. That is where the stars live within you, the constellations. If you approach a person in the immeasurable void or emptiness and pour your intent into their constellations, you will move them. A shift begins to occur. The stars move and form anew. Pour the intent of your will and the attention of your mind into that place of inward sky, and you initiate their becoming."

Twin Dreamers leaned back against the cedar post. Her appearance was haunting.

"That is why initiation is the only road for a shaman to follow," Zoila said.

I smiled, thinking of the many ordeals of my own initiation. The road had been bumpy and beset with snares and pitfalls. I had managed to survive and grow. But spiritual lessons are never easy. To become open to the "cosmic" involves an all-out war between the higher self and the foolish, prideful self. Foolish, prideful self wields a mighty sword and cuts every step of the way. I mentioned this to Twin Dreamers.

"Yes, the road to self-realization is steep and treacherous," she said. "You may react and become scared because you sense your vulnerability. You may talk constantly and become angry, but few initiates will listen and realize that new worlds are being born."

"Ho," Zoila said. She embraced Twin Dreamers. They held hands for a long moment. The wind blew and tossed their hair into tangles. Twin Dreamers put her hand over her left breast and so did Zoila.

No one said anything for a long time. We watched the sky, the stars, the yellow moon over the pines. Zoila patted my hand, got up, and unrolled her blankets on the far end of the porch.

"Tonight," Zoila said, "I'm sleeping out here. But I can't wait to get home to my hammock."

We told her good-night, and she was soon curled up, asleep.

Twin Dreamers searched my eyes. "You're a good shaman, Lynn," she said in a quiet, soothing voice. "You have a good heart. The horse spirits like you. Preserve that instinct in yourself." She stood up, carrying her medicine bundle, and leaned over close to my ear. "Horses will come for you. There will be two of them next time. At first you won't recognize them as horses. You will recognize them by their eyes, and you will see them from high up. Don't be afraid to go with them, Lynn. They are the emissaries from far away. That time is coming fast, and you can believe it is not far off. This will be your most difficult trial. You must ride both horses at once. You will believe you are on a comet. Keep going, no matter what. All your emotions will burn off, both love and hate, joy and sorrow. They will take you to the sacred mountains in the east. There you will meet at the campground of shamans. I will be there, too, and the way will be explained to you once more under these advantageous circumstances."

"What are you saying to me, Twin Dreamers?"

"I'm saying that for you there is another chance. Most people don't exist in their own mind, but you do. That makes it possible for you one day to become a shape shifter." She bent closer and kissed me on the forehead. She stood erect, walked a few steps, then turned back and giggled. She mimicked my expression in such a silly way that I started to laugh too.

"Don't eat moths," she said, still giggling.

"What do you mean?"

"It is that time of night. It is good to be quiet, or the moths fly into your mouth."

I laughed to myself, and Twin Dreamers laughed out loud. She turned and walked away once more, her slight figure melting into the shadows of the poplar trees as she disappeared into the night. A jet of wind blew across my face. A coyote barked several times. The yellow crescent moon emerged from a cloud bank.

I started to rise, but as I did so, something fell off my lap and clattered onto the plank boards of the porch. I searched around and saw the ivory figure. It had landed in such a way that it was standing on its hind legs, rearing up. I knelt so I could see it better. It was stark, frozen in time. I must have looked at it for several minutes. Twin Dreamers had left this horse with me for a reason. I held it in my left palm and then to my cheek.

I knew Twin Dreamers was gone.

16

A Sorcerer's Smoke

One morning after I had finished cleaning the cabin, I decided to take a walk. I told Agnes this.

She was sitting at her wooden table, a haystack of newly picked herbs of every variety mounded in front of her. The previous night Zoila, Ruby, Agnes, and I had prowled around the prairie under the light of the moon and gathered different species of grasses, healing flowers, and herbs. Each time Agnes took a plant, she described its uses to Zoila. We would leave a turquoise bead the size of a button in the hole where the root had been.

"These are medicine flowers," she said. "And that's the price we pay for them. It's small enough, considering their benefits. Never take a child of the sacred soil without paying for it, whether it's with tobacco or a bead. Leave something of your thanks to the plant world."

Now she was tying and hanging the herbs from the rafters in small and large bundles.

"See this proud lady?" Agnes held up a handful of dark green stick grass. "This will make four large boiling kettles of tea. The Hopi peoples are fond of a relative of hers. They call her *hohosi*. It's my favorite beverage. Take the trail up behind the cabin on your walk and pick some more."

"Of course." I took a couple of sticks of the grass to make sure I could identify it. I put it in the breast pocket of my khaki shirt. I folded an old piece of newspaper that I could use to roll the newly picked grass in and put that in my back pocket.

I was happy to do this chore, as I was feeling restless and needed some exercise. I told Agnes I would be a couple of hours and left.

Outside the air was cool, except in the large pools of sunshine. The wind carried the suggestion that autumn was not far off. I jogged briskly, the chilling air seeping through my clothes. The yellow sweater that Shirley, the Cree girl in the secondhand store, had given me was tied loosely around my shoulders. I untied it and slid it on over my khaki shirt. I wondered how Shirley was and if I would ever see her again.

I ran, following the trail and carefully watching for the *hohosi*-like grass. The rhythm of running was like a song. Occasionally I would gaze about at the wealth of scenery around me, the yellow and green shelf grasses bending in the wind, the twisted trees, and the infinite sky. I was not used to running, so I would stop and take short rests, sitting down beside the trail.

I finally found a growth of the grass Agnes wanted. It was bristling in the wind, poking up from the bare earth in clumps. I used my pocketknife and cut low, stacking the long, needlelike stems in the center of the unfolded newspaper, which I had spread out on the ground by my knee. When I had gathered all the newspaper would hold, I carefully folded it up and placed the roll in my belt under my sweater. Then I left some cornmeal for the spirit of the plants.

As I turned on the trail to go back to Agnes's cabin, I caught sight of chimney smoke rising above a saddle of land in the distance. My whole body shivered. Glancing up, I also saw a thunderhead throwing a shadow over the wide grassland. I had not noticed it before, but the thin corkscrew of smoke was clearly visible against its dark background. The only cabin in that direction belonged to Red Dog. I let out a gasp and, clutching my newspaper herb bundle to my stomach, I bolted. I ran all the way back to Agnes's, bursting through the door when I finally reached the cabin.

Agnes looked up from her work at the table and stared at me.

"Agnes, there's smoke coming from Red Dog's cabin!" I was breathing hard, my chest heaving for air.

"Did you bring the tea?" She leaned back against the log wall on two legs of her chair. She was relaxed and smiling.

I was still completely out of breath and unable to speak another word. I sat down in a chair and placed the rolled newspaper in front of her. She reached across the table and opened it. She looked at the cut grass contents and gathered a handful.

"Oh, this is wonderful," she said. She smelled a stem and rolled it between her fingers. "Its virtues are well contained."

I got up and closed the door, which I had neglected to shut because of my excitement. When I turned around, I said, "Agnes, didn't you hear me? Red Dog must be back!" Although I was not cold, I was both shivering and covered with perspiration.

Agnes gave a little exasperated nod of her head as though the whole subject were boring and not worth discussing. She began to weave stems of the *hohosi*-like grass together, tying them in twisted bunches. The result was something that looked like several gray-green shoelaces tied together in a bow. No sooner was one done than she quickly tied another. She began laying out a row of the tied grasses on top of one corner of the unfolded newspaper. I was still breathing heavily. There was a sweet, pungent smell from all the herbs.

I was exasperated and gave a loud sigh. "Red Dog," I said.

Finally, Agnes looked up over her work and said, "Mm, the doggie is back, is he? With his tail between his legs, no doubt. Things are looking up."

"What do you mean, looking up? It's terrible!"

"We have recently wounded his cunning and his pride just as if we had tied a string of firecrackers to his tail. Now, slowly, things will return to normal of their own accord." She gave me the impression that she was totally unconcerned. "Did you think Red Dog would never crawl back home to his own kennel?"

"Well, no. Yes...I don't know," I said lamely, realizing how incoherent I was being. I feebly struggled to say, "I mean, you did play quite a trick on him."

"Yes, he belittled our power by following our trail. He made it a challenge. But we deluded him in the end." She reached for more stems of grass. A smile played across her face, and she really started to giggle. "Those guys sure ran for the hills."

"It looked like their pants were on fire," I said. I couldn't help but smile too.

"They had ants in their pants."

"Yeah, it was pretty funny, all right."

We both broke into a long series of giggles. I was remembering the scene. The mighty and dangerous sorcerer Red Dog and his two trained apprentices had gone berserk. Agnes had tricked them, but I still did not understand how.

"What did you do to Red Dog, Agnes? I never understood."

Agnes pressed another shoestring bundle onto her gathering pile. She looked at me solemnly. "There are two kinds of death, Lynn. I'm speaking in a general way, for in truth there are an infinite number of deaths. But for our purposes I will reduce them to two. There is sudden death and there is friendly death. In a friendly death, Death walks up and greets you. You say hello. You maybe have a smoke and discuss the weather. It's like meeting with an old friend of great power and intelligence. You realize he can open and close the door. No one else can do that. You walk out with him, and he closes the door behind you. That door is closed forever, and you can never return through it again."

"And what about sudden death?" I asked.

"Sudden Death is a stalker. He leaps out on you and forces you through the doorway immediately. Sudden Death is a watcher, an observer. He waits for your most vulnerable time. He shows up at the most unexpected hour. He leaves you banging at the closed doorway trying to get back inside. But you never will. You may cry and beg forever to no avail."

"And what does that have to do with Red Dog?"

"Normally a man like Red Dog is fearless and unafraid of death. He has made his bargain with Death and expects Death to keep his promise to him. Death has promised to forewarn him of his comings and goings."

"What does that have to do with the thing you threw in Red Dog's truck?"

"That thing, as you call it, is known as the broken treaty with Death. It puts you on notice that Death may have you immediately. In this instance his death was busy somewhere else. I made sure of that. But had Death been in the vicinity, all bets would have been off where Red Dog was concerned. As it was, he had to use all his powers to set up a smoke screen so Death wouldn't find him. Believe me, this is not easily accomplished. Even Red Dog would not have stood a chance if Death had been lurking nearby. Red Dog knew immediately what landed in the bed of his pickup."

"That's a pretty good trick, Agnes."

"Yes, one to be careful with and to use only in times of great danger. It's nothing compared with what he was prepared to do to us."

"Well, you certainly turned the tables on him, Agnes. I'll say that."

We had another good laugh, but the idea that Red Dog was so near still made me nervous. I would now have to be on the alert and not take anything for granted.

Agnes set to work in earnest, tying, stacking, and arranging herbs.

"Why are you working so hard to gather all these herbs, Agnes? It seems like you've got more than usual."

"Because I want to give several of these children to Zoila before she leaves. Many of these herbs cannot be found in the south. She can use them in her healing practice."

The thought of Zoila leaving distressed me, because I did not know when I would see her again. "When is Zoila going?" I asked.

"We are going to Ruby's tomorrow night for a goodbye feast."

"Tomorrow night," I whined. I got up and found my medicine bundle. I unwrapped it and got a sandhill crane feather that I had been beading for Zoila. "I'm always the last to know anything," I said. "Thanks for telling me."

In my haste to hurry with the beading of the feather, I pricked my finger. "Ouch!" I cried loudly. Amused, Agnes looked up, her black eyes dancing in the light. Her dignity was most remarkable. Those incredible eyes pierced right through me, and she read instantly the source of my discomfort.

She said in a tone of kindness, "I love Zoila too. And I will think of her, as I often think of Twin Dreamers."

I said simply, "I know."

I returned to my beadwork. I became aware of the smell of the herbs and grasses that surged up with each deep pungent breath. The aroma was rich and savory.

"There is a sweet fragrance that has just enveloped you," Agnes said, looking directly at me. "There, for a moment, you were quiet inside and happy. You had ceased your longing for Arion, for Twin Dreamers. Lately you are always in the process of becoming. The process of becoming finished, of becoming successful, of becoming a shamaness, of becoming sad over losing someone from your life. What happened to now? Your life exists in the shadows of your becoming."

"I don't know."

"Now doesn't exist, because you don't completely accept who you are right now. You think you will accept yourself when Twin Dreamers returns or when you become a better recognized or a better shamaness. But none of this is true. Nothing is ever enough if you don't accept yourself right this moment as complete. If you don't, there will always be a sense of longing, and you will die with that longing even if you are a famous writer or invincible as a healer."

I adjusted myself nervously in my chair. "You're right, Agnes," I said. "I do get uncentered and forget what I'm doing and why." I threaded a row of beads with the needle. Looking at the various colors—black, white, and red—I reflected on what Agnes had said. I asked, "Is that why a person can spend her whole life building extraordinary success and then, when she is truly rich and famous, she is even more miserable?"

Agnes was silent, wrapping and tying an herb bundle. She looked at me and said, "Yes, in part. There could be many reasons. Emotional suffering is a big disguiser, a mask. Suffering can be a kind of arrogant belligerence with which you agonize through life. Take off that mask, and the person has lost her main occupation. So no matter what she accomplishes, she will be wearing that false face. She will simply give it another name.

"If you are always becoming your whole life through, and suddenly there is nothing left to become, you are filled with terror. Because becoming is your life distraction, and suddenly you are face-to-face with your own empty being. It's like sitting down to a great feast and realizing it is a banquet for the dead. And you are the only one eating. You want to run from the feast, but where are you to go?"

Agnes stood up and placed several herb bundles in my lap. She pointed at a row of nails along a rafter above my head. I hung each one separately. Afterward I got a rope of sweetgrass from my bundle. I tied some red yarn around the end of the rope and presented it to Agnes. She took it approvingly, clucked her tongue, and said, "Let's have some tea. This new batch will be good."

The next day was spent preparing to go to Ruby's for Zoila's farewell feast. Early in the morning I had picked more blackberries. I kept remembering Twin Dreamers and seeing her face looking up, through the entwined brambles. How I wished she were with us, with her odd smile and twinkling eyes, her sedate wisdom. When I got back to the cabin, Agnes and I made some sweet bread and a large bowl of wild asparagus salad. Our most ambitious project was a deer sausage pie, which turned out well, with just the right amount of garlic and other seasonings. It took us an hour or more to wrap the herbs for Zoila in special red fabric bundles. Late in the afternoon July arrived in the truck to pick us up. Agnes and I were in a festive mood. July was excited about being able to travel south with Zoila. This I hadn't known or expected, and I was slightly envious. Ruby, it seemed, had sprung it on her at the last minute.

"I think the plant children are my way," July announced happily. "Ruby is sharing me with Zoila. When next I see you, I should know something, Lynn."

"That's wonderful, July," I said. "Zoila can teach you a great deal. You certainly are fortunate, but I'll miss you."

We embraced for a moment.

"The magical herbs and sacred plants of Guatemala and the Yucatan will test your skills, July," Agnes said. "Approach these children in all humility. Though you were born in the north, you are a south person."

"I won't be gone for more than a few months," July said.

We gathered up the food and gifts and laughed all the way to the truck. We got in and drove over to Ruby's. When we walked into her cabin, I was not prepared for what I saw. Zoila had hunted a deer. An altar had been erected against the east log wall. Sage smoke billowed up from a clay dish on the left. The five-point deer antlers and head rose up out of a large cooking pot. It had obviously been simmering all day but was now placed in the center of the altar to receive offerings. Pieces of colored ribbons, feathers, and hand-written prayers hung from the pronged antlers as gifts to the spirit of the deer. Two candles burned on either side of the cooking pot. Slabs of deer meat had been wrapped and set out prominently, while most of the innards had been stewed in the pot.

Entering, we placed our food and gifts on the altar. Ruby handed Agnes and me deer-foot rattles and gave a drum to July. Zoila and July drummed, and Agnes and I shook the rattles in tempo, while Ruby sang her lightning song to the deer's spirit. She covered the pot momentarily with the newly skinned deer hide. Agnes motioned for me to follow her. We both put feathers and herb bundles on the antlers and chanted our prayers as we burned more cedar and sweetgrass.

Soon afterward we were all seated, prepared to eat a proper feast. Ruby gave the blessing. "The spirit of the deer is our spirit. He gave away that we may have life. In honor of the deer and of our sister Zoila, we celebrate this evening."

We had waited all day for this repast. Between bites I watched the copper-colored faces of the medicine women. I felt proud to be in their company. We all ate heartily. Smoke from the cedar and sage was a grayish color in the candlelight. After the meal Zoila looked at her gifts. I had given her a bottle of perfume and the crane feather. She seemed pleased with both. I was surprised that Agnes and Ruby gave July and Zoila two twenty-dollar bills each. It was a lot of money for them to give. Then they looked at me expectantly. I was embarrassed and forked over two fifty-dollar bills.

"It's called *chandi*," Agnes said. "It's an old tradition to help the travelers on their way."

"It's for luck," Ruby added. "A custom with great practical value."

We had herb tea from the gourd cups with the dessert course. We slowly ate the blackberry pie and talked. The mood changed as the party wound to a close. We all set to work clearing the table. When we finished, Ruby was standing in front of the huge stack of bowls, pots, and dishes that stood in the sink.

Ruby said, "Lynn, you stay tonight and help July with her things. Also, these dishes must be washed and put away. But first, July, let's ride over to Agnes's and drop her off."

"Okay, I'll walk home in the morning," I said. I rolled up my sleeves and scraped the scraps from the pink-flowered plates into the compost barrel. Then I turned my attention to the bowls and the scullery work. Every dish, jelly jar, pot, pan, and utensil was dirty.

They all filed out of the cabin to July's truck, leaving me alone. "We'll try to get back in time to help you, Lynn," Ruby said, going out the door.

When July, Ruby, and Zoila returned I was just putting the finishing touches on the cleanup. Ruby did not compliment my diligence. We all went to bed without a word.

17

Shifting the World

The next morning I awoke slowly, tracing every water stain and knothole in the ceiling with my bloodshot eyes. I had not slept well on the floor. Lazily I drifted in and out of sleep, listening to the drowsy hum of the green-headed flies outside the screen windows. Suddenly the cabin door opened with a thud from Ruby's booted foot. The hinges screeched a complaint and splinters of bark and wood flew in all directions as Ruby stomped over with a large armful of wood and dumped it in a crate beside the potbellied stove.

"Good morning, everybody," Ruby said loudly in an exacerbated voice. "Where's my breakfast?"

I saw July's eyelids snap open like two switchblades. She was up and dressed in moments. I sat up brushing wood chips off the sleeping bag I had borrowed and struggled to stand.

"A true warrioress this morning, Lynn." Ruby bent and snatched the sleeping bag, rolled it up, and stowed it under her bed before I could even bend down to help.

"Lynn, why don't you make us all some cornmeal mush?" Ruby asked. "Would that be agreeable with you, or would you rather I help you to a chair?"

"Well, thank you for the offer, Ruby," I said. "But I'll be fine if you'll just give me a minute to wash my face."

She gave me a friendly shove. "All right, but be quick about it."

Zoila came in while I was washing my face. She patted me on the back.

It was a companionable enough breakfast. But as I ate my corn mush and sipped on my sage tea, I was saddened. I knew it would be a long time until I would see either Zoila or July again. Zoila had said we would meet again soon in *el foral*, the light. We said goodbye with tears in our eyes. Ruby and I waved as July pulled her pickup out onto the dirt road.

I did a few odd jobs for Ruby, said goodbye, and set off up the trail to Agnes's cabin. After a while I left the usual path and followed a tiny stream that ran swift and clear. Then I walked up across an overhanging ridge of hard granite. I knelt down to sift through slivers of flint strewn around here and there. There were a few pieces that looked as if they had been worked by human hands. I sorted them out and put them in the pocket of my jeans along with the horse figure.

My pocket bulging, I set off again, walking along the ridge. I noticed a cluster of old, storm-torn pine trees in front of me near the path's edge. Lightning had struck two of them at mid-trunk, splitting the upper portion. The trunks and dried limbs protruded out over the path. The weather had taken its toll, shriveling and distorting the once-rich boughs. The sight was spectral, like hovering ghostly travelers from another dimension. I stopped. There was something unfamiliar and treacherous about those trees. Their branches reached overhead like writhing snakes in the wind.

I had walked this path for ten years, and for some unknown reason I had never noticed these pine trees before. Perhaps the lightning had recently disturbed them. I did not want to walk anywhere near the grove. Instead I walked around in a wide arc through the brushwood. I got bunches of cheat grass stuck in my socks. The darkening clouds gathered above me, and I saw three large beetle-black ravens perched along a cedar branch up ahead of me. A splinter of lightning shattered the gray-and-purple sky. The thunder roll made me jump as it slammed overhead.

The path began to seem peculiar. I attributed this to the startling lightning. The shadows, the light, even the bushes appeared more scraggly and stark against the buff-colored background of dried weeds and grasses. The wind shifted. The air turned crisp and cold. Obviously, I was going to get caught in a downpour. I started to run, the cheat grass annoying me, digging into the skin on my ankles. I paused, sitting on a bare rock. I laboriously picked the foxtails out of my flesh one by one. As I stood up, large drops of rain were pelting down on top of my head.

I pulled my sweater up around my throat and cursed my luck. I had forgotten to bring a rain poncho. I jogged for a hundred paces or so and stopped in my tracks. I remembered seeing the sky before leaving Ruby's. It had been clear blue, with a few ruffled patches of naked clouds. There had not been any sign of rain, and the air had been tranquil. According to my watch, that had been only an hour and a half ago. Then I realized that my watch, which had always kept perfect time, had stopped. The icy rain peppered down, raising tiny wisps of dust as the drops struck the dry land. My hair became wet and plastered to my head. I began to run again. I was wet through and through and cold. I rounded a turn in the trail and came upon an escarpment of red jasper stone. The angular formation was jagged and grotesque in the flat, darkened light. I stopped again. Rivulets of rainwater were dripping off my nose and chin.

Nothing on this trail looked right. I squatted down and peered up at the harsh jasper spires above me. I had no recollection of such rocks jutting out in an odd formation. I was completely disoriented. For a moment I was totally lost, and I began to cry. How could I be so confused? And what was the matter with me, behaving in such an indulgent way? I knew this land perfectly well. I grasped the horse in my pocket for strength and stood up. Taking a deep earth-scented breath, I continued.

Around the next turn I was relieved to see the path was recognizable. The trees and the hills were in familiar positions. With enormous relief I saw smoke rising beyond the treetops and knew it had to be from Agnes's cabin.

The rain lessened as I ran swiftly down the trail. In no time at all I was up on the porch and then closing the door behind me. I was wet and tired and must have looked pretty bad. I kicked off my sneakers and called to Agnes. There was no answer. I wondered where she could have been. She knew I was to return immediately after Zoila and July left. But the cabin was empty. The light seemed dimmer than usual. I went to the stove to warm my hands. I held them over the top, but there was no warmth. I opened the door and peered inside. The belly was filled with glowing coals. When I pulled the door back, the flames leapt out at me. I held my hands close once more, but still there was no heat coming from the fire.

"That's positively insane," I said.

Standing in a widening puddle, I tore off my clothes. I grabbed for the towel hanging by the sink, but there was a buck knife hanging there instead.

"Agnes, where did you put my towel?" I said to myself.

I thought maybe the buck knife was Ruby's. I had never examined hers for any length of time.

"Well, you've seen one knife…" I said under my breath.

I turned and went for my clothes in the cedar chest. Where the cedar chest had been, there was a Hudson Bay blanket folded and resting on a chair. Agnes had rearranged everything. I did not see the cedar chest anywhere. I took the blanket and wrapped myself in it. I did not recognize the blanket either. It had a red, yellow, and black stripe on both ends. The wool was prickly against my skin, but at least it was dry.

I walked over and sat down in my customary chair at the table. I almost lurched to the floor when I realized that the chairs and table were different and had been moved to the other side of the stove. Agnes must have completely changed everything. I wondered where she had put my clothes? I was becoming distressed and wished Agnes would return soon to explain the new order of things. Even the log walls, the windows, the furniture seemed changed. I moved to another chair and sat down very cautiously. What was happening here? My heart skipped a beat, and I pulled the blanket tighter around myself. I did not feel well. I had been ignoring a terrible pressure at the back of my neck.

"If you have a cup of tea, Lynn," I said to myself, "you will feel better. You will be able to think." I went over to the cupboard, reached for my usual cup, and turned the camp stove on at the same time.

As my fingers curled around the cup handle, I felt something bristly like a soft brush. Then slowly it started to move.

I jumped back, clattering into the table, and screamed from my very blood. The face of Red Dog was in my hand, and my fingers were clutching his red beard. The face didn't go away. Instead, his form filled out. He was standing right in front of me! His tall, muscular body uncoiled like a snake from out of the cupboard and shelves. Then I realized I was not in Agnes's cabin at all. I was in Red Dog's cabin!

I cut loose with another impotent scream. Red Dog's head was thrown back in a loud, raucous laugh. His eyes pierced me like darts striking a dartboard. Half scrambling, half running, I tumbled headlong for the door. Inside my head and down my neck there was an impact as if something had snapped back into place. Red Dog's laughter lived like an explosion in my head. My fingers clawed at the door latch, but, of course, it was locked.

Red Dog grabbed my arm and threw me against the opposite wall, and I smashed a chair and several boxes in my fall. I sat up on the floor against the log wall and huddled in my blanket. I watched Red Dog's face, half in fascination and half in terror. His eyes were pinpoints of red light and his mouth hung open like that of some enormous fish waiting to suck a squirming worm off a hook. His eyes stared at my body, my face. But his gaze was not sexual. He wanted something more. He wanted my innards, my nourishing power. He wanted to draw the life force from my body, leaving me a dead thing, my skin like the deer hide at Ruby's, an inanimate covering. A slow smile broke like the sun through storm clouds over his dark expression. His uneven teeth glinted, predatory and smoke-stained in the sparse light from the window. I was paralyzed. I just sat there, a shivering mud lark in shock.

He pulled up a chair and put his boots on the table. Opening his Bull Durham with his teeth, he slaked a measure of tobacco onto a paper. He casually rolled a cigarette. He lit it with a wooden match scratched over his jeans.

"I don't know how you can be such a pathetic, stupid woman, and yet . . ." He took a drag, blowing smoke rings toward the log rafters. "You are powerful in your strange way. It must be because you are a civilized white. It takes power like yours to be fooled so completely. You're too smart for your own good. You can't find your way out of the maze. If you would work with me, you would see real beauty and you would know true power. I mean power like the power from a million suns. Those women over there don't know their asses from holes in the ground. Oh, sure. Those hags can do a few tricks. But tricks are one thing. My kind of power is something else."

"What happened to me?" I asked. "Is this really your cabin?"

He snarled sarcastically, "No, it's Ruby's, you idiot!"

"You're very good, Red Dog. You have managed to disorient me and make me lose my way. Such a noble use of your power. What unimaginable beauty you have shown me." My fear was gone, and a cold, calculating anger was welling up from within the deepest part of me. I despised this man and I feared him. But he had done a job on me I would not soon forget. I wanted to know how. It is a monumental task to trick a wolf, or one with wolf medicine such as mine, into losing her way. I had a kind of morbid curiosity about what he had done to me.

"You want to know how I did it, don't you?"

"Yes," I answered. "It's like you moved our known world, shifted it somewhere else."

"No, I shifted you, little Miss Shape-Shifter."

"How . . ." I started to ask him how he knew about my apprenticeship in shape shifting but stopped myself.

"You fool. I can read your mind. I know what you're doing any time I want to know. If you had any power I could use, I would rip it right out of you. But you don't. You don't understand the profiles of real beauty. You think those muddle-brained broken-down old Indians— women, of all things—have the answer."

He looked so demented, I was afraid to open my mouth. He got up from his chair, leaned over to me, and said, "Boo!"

I drew back in fear, and he turned away. He took a brown apothecary jar from a shelf and started rubbing some kind of glistening oil on his red, parched hands. He put the jar away and wiped his hands on his jeans. He sat back down and looked at me in a disapproving manner. "Simple," he said. "For me. I compelled you here. I got inside your tiny little mind with that flint you picked up. If you had been smart, you would have seen it was not of native material. It called to you from the stars. Look at it closely and you'll see that it is not flint at all, but a meteorite. Meteors are my allies. Chips of stars, they work for me."

"But how?"

"How? It compelled you to its owner. Me! Mine!" He tapped his chest with his thumb. "But it also fooled your eyes into seeing what I wanted you to see. It took you back in time. Many years ago, this cabin belonged to Agnes. Your instinct knew the scent of Agnes was here from long ago. You see, until you saw me, your mind was still back there playing with those flints. Or what you thought were flints. You felt a current in your neck and head. That was to alter you. I moved the current around to both destroy old regions and manifest new ones."

His words permeated me with cold, naked dread. I was not sure what his explanation meant, but I knew it was bad. My apprehension built with each moment that passed.

"One day you will begin to understand humble power. I'm the best. I guess wrong every once in a while. I guessed wrong in the Yucatan. After that business with Jaguar Woman, I went farther south to Peru. I met an old sorcerer friend, and he showed me some powers from the ancient ways. Methods to move stone, people, ways to change the structure of the earth, beginning at the core, the magma. Yes, Lynn, I can cause the earth itself to convulse and tremble and shake. To do this

I have to join with other sorcerers. I wish I could do this alone, but the snake must bite its tail to release this synergistic energy. We sorcerers planned to make your days in California limited. But we could only raise slight tremors. Your sisters were blocking the way. Unfortunately the so-called sisterhood prevented the destruction that we initiated. But we will prevail. Your circle can never last. You have a big ego. All you puny women do. Before long you will break up and stop your nonsense."

I was aghast at his declaration of intent. Egos, indeed! How this man looked at the Sisterhood of the Shields through his own distorted veils.

"Red Dog," I said, "do you mean to tell me that you are using your power to create natural disasters, like earthquakes?"

"Yes, and certain governments are even paying us big money."

"I don't believe you."

"Of course, you don't," he said. He laughed. "You're ignorant. That's why I'm telling you. Hey, I always let you go, don't I? You are amazing in your futility. Eventually I'll destroy you. I'll do that in my own time and in my own way. First I want to have some fun. You white-lighters are all the same. You think you can cure the people of this world with love. Nonsense. It takes more than that. It takes getting rid of a few million of the sniveling bastards first. And it will just look like your precious Mama Earth did it all by herself." He started to laugh again. This time he laughed until he was frothing spittle from the corners of his mouth.

Red Dog was even more diabolical than I had imagined. And he seemed positively insane. He filled me with such loathing and disgust, I could hardly breathe. I began to wonder if he could possibly be telling the truth.

"What governments?" I asked, my voice barely audible.

"Oh, no, you don't." He leapt to his feet. "Don't you know I can see right through you? I know what you had for breakfast." He picked up my clothes and threw them at me.

"You have such a bad opinion of me," he said. "I was just fooling around. You overreacted, as you always do. You concluded in your ignorance that I'm going to hurt you. I wouldn't kill anybody. Even you. That would be too easy. Besides, then what would I do for fun?"

I put my wet clothes back on, underneath the blanket.

"Give me my blanket and flint back," he bellowed. "Unless, of course, you'd like to come back tomorrow for tea."

I searched through my pockets and emptied the flint pieces onto the table, careful not to expose the ivory horse. I tried not to even think about it, so he could not perceive it by reading my mind. He might want to use the horse figure as a pathway to get to Twin Dreamers.

"I'm done with you. I want you to leave," he said, dismissing me.

I folded the blanket and draped it on the chair where I had found it. Red Dog opened the door for me. "Make tracks, lady."

He did not have to tell me twice. I ran to Agnes's cabin in a fury.

18

The Fire Spirit

Back at the cabin, Agnes had smeared me with a pungent-smelling salve, wrapped me in hot towels, and put me to bed. She had refused to discuss my experiences. I slept for twelve hours straight. When I got up, I dressed in warm clothes and sat down for tea. The brew was not the usual drink Agnes served. This concoction was bitter and seemed to have a reviving quality.

"Will you talk about Red Dog now?" I asked.

"No. Red Dog is an evil, stupid man. I knew where you were. I also knew he would not harm you. I wanted you to see his unadorned malignancy. One day he will be caught in his own tangled web."

I questioned Agnes further, but she would only say, "It's a waste of breath." She finally forbade me to speak further of my experiences.

Late in the evening, Ruby joined us. She was in her usual contrary mood. "Coming over here," she said, "I saw a black dog walking upright. I don't know who it was. But whenever you see that, you immediately know it's a black sorcerer on the prowl. He must scent something tasty."

She then gave me a long lecture about how July had deserted her. "What do you think of someone leaving an old blind person like that? Pretty low, I'd say."

"But, Ruby, you told July to go."

"No, I didn't. I only told her to go to test her loyalty. Sure enough, she deserted me."

"Ruby, that's not true," I said. "July or I would do anything for you."

"Is that so?" Ruby said. "Well, there are certain things, now that you mention it, that need to be done." She proceeded to list enough jobs to fill the next several years. "And after my cabin is electrified, I want a television, a microwave oven, and a stereo record player to listen to while I'm talking to my girl chums on the telephone."

I reluctantly agreed to all her demands. On that note, I went to bed.

We awoke to a loud banging sound. Someone was knocking on the cabin door. Ruby had spent the night with us, and we were jolted out of our deep sleep. Streamers of dawn's light filtered in through the irregular window. When I sat up in my sleeping bag, the sky shone with a milky blue, a cool mist still caught in the low branches of the trees. Agnes had thrown on a skirt, sweater, and jacket, and now she was answering the door.

"Well, David Carson. You finally made it," Agnes said.

I saw them talking together in a low voice. Carson was framed against the opalescent light.

Agnes went to a chair, leaving him standing in the doorway. She put on a pair of moccasins and went out on the porch with Carson, closing the door behind her.

Ruby got up, grumbling. I did not understand her.

"What did you say, Ruby?"

"I said that blasted David Carson. The last time he was up here in the north, he camped out over by my cabin. He invited himself to breakfast, lunch, and dinner and ate everything in sight. And drank everything. He just thinks he can horn in whenever he wants. It's just like him. I was sleeping soundly."

"He's traveled a long way," I offered tentatively. I was weary and annoyed myself. "Isn't he from Oklahoma?"

"They say he is. But I think it's a lie. Anyone rude enough to interrupt a good dream couldn't be from a nice place like Oklahoma. A good dream is worth more than any man. Besides, he could have called."

I smiled to myself. There was not a telephone anywhere in the vicinity. Ruby was clomping around, putting on her clothes. I followed her example, washing up and dressing. I put on some water for tea. Agnes and Carson came inside, leaving the cabin door open to the brisk morning air.

"Got anything to eat around here?" Carson asked. "I'm so hungry I could eat the rear end off a buffalo."

Agnes told me to make some breakfast.

We all sat around and ate.

"I'd have been here sooner, Ruby," Carson said. "I knew you missed me. But I had trouble with my truck."

"What kind of trouble?" I asked.

"Damned thing stopped at every saloon between here and Oklahoma," he said, pushing himself back in his chair and tilting it against the log walls. "I'll have to get it fixed, I guess."

I told him the story Ben had told me in Santa Barbara about his experiences as his apprentice.

"I teach power the old-fashioned way," Carson said. "You earn it."

We all laughed, and Ruby said, "Well?"

"Oh, okay, Ruby." Carson nodded.

He went out to his truck. When he had come back inside and seated himself again, he placed three wrapped leather bundles on the tabletop.

"Ruby, I've brought what you asked for," Carson said.

Looking at David Carson, I was surprised by his resemblance to Red Dog. Although he was shorter and did not have the demeanor of evil about him, he did have the same unkempt red hair and scraggly beard. He could have been Red Dog's brother, but his eyes held a different kind of light. They held the wisdom of the eagle, piercing and predatory. He carefully unwrapped the bundles one by one. Each bundle contained a herkamer crystal that scintillated like a diamond. The crystals had a quality of light I had never seen before. They were four-inch-long wands, heavy and faceted at both ends. In the center of each crystal was a perfect triangle or pyramid with what appeared to be a flame of red and yellow contained within it.

Agnes and Ruby both held up the crystals, one by one, to the light.

"Look, Lynn," Agnes said. "If you hold the crystals just right, you can see the sacred fire burning in the pyramid." She handed me the one she had been examining. I held it up and turned it slowly in a ray of light from the window. I found the pristine shadow of a pyramid with a feather of scarlet inside. I caught my breath. It was exquisite. When I turned it in my hand, it was a living flame. I wondered why this man had been entrusted with crystals so powerful and sacred.

"You have brought us the correct crystals from the grandmothers," Agnes said. "You are a trusted courier. If you could not have come, we would not have had the crystals in time."

"It's about time you did something right, Carson," Ruby said.

"Got anything else to eat?" Carson asked. He had cleaned his plate twice.

"No, we don't," Ruby said.

"Those crystals have kept me awake for days," he said. "Got any place to sleep?"

"You can check into a motel when you get to Winnipeg," Ruby said.

"What do you use these crystals for?" I asked.

"These crystals are like shooting stars," Agnes answered. "They are called traveling crystals."

"Well, they sure kept me traveling," Carson said.

Agnes was still inspecting them, fondling each one. She turned to Ruby. "Is this runner yours?"

She handed the crystal to Ruby, laying the wand in her brown, calloused palm. Ruby held it, closing her eyes.

She said, "No, this is not her."

Ruby put it back down on the table and then immediately picked up another. She closed her eyes again and soon said, "Yes, I have found her. This is the old one, and it's been a long time."

Carson lit up a cigarette. I was sitting next to him, and it seemed as though he were blowing the smoke in my direction. I did not say anything about it, because I did not want to offend him. With his tangled red hair and darting blue eyes, he looked like an inhabitant of some storybook world. Both Agnes and Ruby were holding crystals. It was as if the crystals were old friends, and they stroked them familiarly.

I coughed, and Carson said, "Excuse me." He put out his cigarette.

Agnes handed me the largest of the three crystals. "This one must belong to Lynn."

I closed my eyes and held it in my left hand for a long moment. It was cool and smooth and felt good. I nodded my head approvingly and opened my eyes with a big smile.

Carson suddenly turned and was quickly on his feet. "Well, ladies, I'm on my way back down south," he said. "Who is going to give me my two hundred and eighty dollars for traveling expenses?"

Agnes and Ruby looked at me. I paid him with three hundred-dollar bills from my suitcase. He was not able to make change, so he kept the extra twenty dollars. I was glad to do it, considering the three beautiful crystals.

We all walked Carson onto the porch with many thanks. Agnes and Ruby both hugged him, and I think even Ruby was sad to see him go. Just as he started up the trail to his pickup truck, he turned and looked directly at me. His eyes were a cadmium blue and held mine like a vise. "Lynn, don't be afraid to follow the crystal." Before I could say anything, he turned and disappeared around the bend in the trail.

I stood there for a moment and then said, "What did he mean by that?"

"Oh, just one of Carson's enigmatic statements, fringed with riddles," Agnes answered. She averted her gaze and went back into the cabin with Ruby following at her heels.

When I got inside, Ruby did something unexpected. She put her arm around me and looked at me lovingly. "We are all given life on this earth by the Great Spirit. The Great Spirit also gave us a central flame.

By that I mean that there is a center within each of us. You cannot live without this center. But only a few shamans and special people are aware that it exists. Hold up your crystal and see how you have to turn it just to see the flames catch. That is the position you occupy in life. You have to travel within and situate yourself in a certain way before the flame can even be seen, much less felt. The flame inside of you was ignited at birth and provides a bridge between you and the Great Spirit. To experience this central flame is to understand your place in the stars. The universe in all its mystery and beauty is your flame."

"I don't understand," I said.

"Come, let's go for a walk," Ruby said.

We were soon walking up the trail, and Ruby still had her hand on my shoulder. Ruby stooped and smelled a yellow wildflower and indicated that I should do the same. I bent, cupping the flower in my hand.

"Just as this sweet flower is unaware of its roots and the source of its life, so are you," Ruby said. "But you have the possibility of knowing your source. The flame within you can grow, and you can learn to tend and care for it."

"But how?" I asked.

Ruby patted me on the back near the base of my spine. "You can become aware of your death. If you cannot see your center flame, you cannot see your death. Knowledge of your death is a gift from the Great Spirit to us all. That flower can never know what you know."

As we walked back to the cabin, I had a view of the meadow with wildflowers blooming up to the foot of the dusky hillside. The bees were working, darting from flower to flower. Ruby still had her arm around my shoulder.

When we came inside the cabin, Agnes was cleaning up the breakfast dishes. She had made the beds and picked up my bedroll. Everything looked tidy and shipshape. Sitting down at the table, I pondered Ruby's words about the importance of living at one's center. She saw this phenomenon as a flame; at least she had described it thus. The sunlight through the poplar leaves created a flickering dapple in the room. I absently picked up one of the three crystals and held it in one spot where the light was favorable. I was nearly hypnotized, just staring at the tiny flame within the pyramid. In the fluttering light there was a dazzle of jeweled flame.

Ruby came over and snatched the crystal out of my hand. She said in a bellicose voice, "Don't wake her. She needs to rest now." She hurriedly put the crystal back inside its pouch. I was surprised at the sudden intrusion on my thoughts. I stared at her vacantly.

"Ruby, you could have just asked me for it," I said. "I would have given it to you. You didn't have to grab it out of my hand."

Agnes and Ruby looked at each other and laughed. They sat down on either side of me. Agnes returned the other two crystals to their pouches. I saw she had a large leather sack on her lap. With a gourd she cupped several measures of cornmeal onto the center of the table until there was a large mound, about three inches high. She smoothed this with her extended fingers and the palm of her hand. Ruby placed a red silk scarf on top of the mound. With great care and ceremony, Agnes laid the three pouches on the scarf. They turned to me. Ruby took my left hand and Agnes took my right.

"What's going on?" I asked. "You're both behaving strangely."

"The crystals are causing this," Agnes said. "They always bring an unusual kind of energy."

"They are obviously important. What kind of crystals are these again?"

"As I have already told you, these are traveling or journeying crystals. These three crystals have been passed down through the Sisterhood of the Shields since ancient times. They are not of this earth. They are a gift from the stars. They are relatives of the constellations that live within you. That place of forgetting and remembering that is your central flame is their sister. They long to be reunited with her."

"Is that what the Maya people call the seat of the jaguar?" I asked.

"Yes, that is what we medicine women call the central fire. What the sorcerers call the crossroads. It is all the same," Agnes informed me.

"You must be consumed by your center. You must pick up the reins of that sacred horse called spirit fire and balance between the positive and the negative forces. As a warrioress, as a woman of power, you must mount the central fire like a horse and unite with the infinite universe." Agnes squeezed my hand.

"But, Agnes, how do I mount a flame like a horse?" I asked, feeling uneasy at her extreme friendliness.

At this question Ruby and Agnes both squeezed my hands affectionately. Agnes thought for a long time, and Ruby just shook her head. I heard the wind outside ruffling the leaves in the treetops. The door suddenly blew open. Ruby released my hand and got up to shut it. She sat back down.

"Lynn," Ruby said, taking my hand once again, "we have no words to explain what is truly sacred. There are no images that demonstrate the process by which we can bring magic out of the great mystery. We can only love you, and within that love and infinite care, we can hope that your own power when enhanced by ours will enable you to experience what language could never explain."

Agnes's and Ruby's faces were a polished copper color in the splashes of light that came into the room from outside the window. Their eyes stared at me. Their withered faces were intent. It struck me how very powerful these two medicine women truly were. I had felt a real shift in their attitude toward me, as if they had elevated me to a higher position in some way.

"I'm feeling funny," I said after a long pause.

"Funny?" Ruby said. "Why, Lynn, that's spoken as the true literary talent you are. Promise me you'll put that in your next book." She stomped her foot and giggled. She pinched the muscle on my upper arm.

Agnes teased me some more. "Ruby, you know she writes because she can't talk. The first few weeks I knew this girl, I couldn't understand a word she said."

"That's nothing," Ruby returned. "I've never been able to understand her. She has the worst accent. I wonder if we have accents to her?"

They both giggled and slapped me on the back, having fun at my expense. Then there was a lingering silence, with only the brisk wind in the trees making a wavering sound. I do not know why, but I felt like crying.

Agnes said, "The night of the ceremony in the cave of Mother Wisdom, you correctly identified the central figure. You were uncertain, but somehow you knew. The sisterhood read your lights that evening, and you have rendered yourself open and ready. I told you once, many years ago, that you have made a bid for power. Power has chosen you as its bride. Tonight we will perform a sacred marriage, and you will unite with that power that has been courting you."

Her words were somewhat heady and frightening. I took a deep breath to quiet my reeling thoughts.

Agnes added, "Power is not monogamous. We are all married to the one source."

"What are you saying to me, Agnes?"

"I am saying that you are not to eat today and that there is to be no more talk. We will take a sweat at sundown. I want you to surround yourself with your medicine bundles and gather power. If you collect enough power, then the gates will burst open."

"Yes, smoke your pipe and pray for wisdom and strength," Ruby said with finality. "You will need it tonight on the sacred mountain." She squeezed my hand a last time and then got up and went outside. Agnes followed her.

I soon heard the sound of the axe chucking heavily on a cedar log. Agnes was chopping wood. I was stunned and apprehensive, wondering what the two medicine women were up to. Soon Ruby came back in with an armload of short logs. She dumped them into the wood box.

"One other thing, Lynn," she said. "Wear your crystal next to your body for several hours. Make her yours. She is different from any other crystal on earth, and she needs only to be near you a short time to understand what you need. She has only been used by the highest order of the sisterhood. She is protected, as you now are protected by her."

I was looking up at her from my chair. Ruby leaned forward and smiled sweetly at me. This act completely unnerved me. She smiled at me as she had one time ten years before. Then, she had just tripped me and sent me sprawling face down in the dirt.

Impulsively I went to my flight bag and rummaged around. I found a carton of cigarettes and placed them in Ruby's hand. To Ruby this was a sacred act, and she held the cigarettes to her heart. She smiled ever so sweetly again. She sensed me trembling in fear, and that sent her into gales of laughter.

The mist was lifting off the ground when the three of us left Agnes's cabin. It was strange weather, with cool, crazy winds that would one minute part the fog and the next let it close in on us in descending gray curtains. First we had a sweat in the sweat lodge. Then we put our clothes back on and set off up the path to the sacred mountain. The mist swirled and lifted, opening to the stars and moon-washed ridges and jumbled boulders. Agnes led the way, and Ruby was behind me. Our movements were sure but slow on the rocky trail. Agnes's dark form would grow large, magnified in the fog-smoked night. The sky was cold and black with a yellow-haloed moon. The stars, when I could see them, were brighter than usual. They shone like brilliant turquoise beads. We walked on an upgrade for more than an hour, then the path leveled out. Ruby moved to my side. I saw her face, and her expression was solemn. Then the grayness folded over her, and her face lost its proportion.

The path turned upward again and went on for about a thousand feet at a slow rise. We were suddenly at the pinnacle of the highest land anywhere in the area. The fog split open, and I saw a ceremonial medicine circle. It had been fashioned hundreds of years ago. A few long, purple-gray cloud wings terraced the sky in front of us. The half moon edged the clouds with a silver iridescence. The moon itself glided in and out of the clouds. The scattered stars were swimming in the black pools of night.

I had known Agnes and Ruby for many years, yet I had never seen them vibrating with such intensely contained force. Neither of them had spoken since morning. They had broken silence only in the sweat lodge to say prayers. The force they were emanating was contagious. Or maybe it was my crystal that was lending me such an extreme form of tension. It was swinging back and forth in its pouch, which hung from a leather thong around my neck. I felt exquisitely alive and sensitive to all life around me. I had always felt close to Agnes and even to Ruby, who could petrify me with fear. As we stood in front of the ancient medicine circle, I was experiencing a different sort of kinship. It was deeper and stronger than it had ever been before. I felt an equilibrium, a string perfectly tuned. I knew instinctively that this clarity was helped by the crystal.

The twelve large stones of the medicine wheel shone white and smooth in the moonlight, occasionally dimming to a lusterless pearl gray. Each of us entered the wheel and closed it at the east doorway. Agnes blessed the wheel with tobacco and cornmeal, and Ruby burned sage, cedar, and sweetgrass. We each made our offerings to the spirit of the place.

Ruby sat in the west, Agnes in the east, and I sat in the north. I settled comfortably on my blanket. The fog-tinged clouds parted again, and I watched Venus sparkling clearly in the jet sky. Then three falling stars arced in a shower of light. Agnes and Ruby began to chant in a guttural language. It sounded Indigenous but was certainly not Cree. Perhaps it was some long-forgotten tongue, for it touched a deep atavistic chord within me. I discovered I was chanting the same words with them, and it all felt perfectly natural.

When the chant was over, Agnes stood and said, "Tonight you will learn that the Great Spirit and the Great Mother have not given you life so that you would be alone. To know that you are truly alone is the first step on a long journey to self-discovery on the path to power. The next step is to learn that you are linked with the universe, that you live in all the lodges of the universe. Life flowers and nourishes itself from within. Beingness has realized itself within you."

She began to draw the different constellations with the cornmeal that she was spreading over the even ground in various lines and characters. She turned her leather sack inside out and shook the last of the meal onto the ground. She worked this up into star symbols until the whole medicine wheel looked like an enormous glowing star chart. She went back to her place in the east. "Lynn," she said, "I may sound like I am contradicting myself, but I am not. It is your language that is contradictory. The only way to understand me is to experience my words. You think that your life has nothing to do with any other life. This is the self-council. In self-council you must separate and become responsible for your own power. This process cuts cords that bleed your much-needed energy. When that is accomplished, a realization occurs. You open to the grand council and the great council fires within. You begin to understand that the galaxies, the mother stars, all existence, in fact, awakens within your own being. In a sense you are all existence. You are the womb from which the stars are born. All life is your firstborn child. The trees, the flowers, and all the creatures of earth have their rootedness in your special being. It does not seem so, but it has always been that way. To know these things, the central council fires of your personal experience must be ignited, and you must warm your hands on your own inner-spirit flame."

I looked out over the stars Agnes had drawn in the circle. I was suddenly aware that they were perfectly matched to the stars in the sky. Agnes was holding her hands prayerlike, and she began to rub her palms back and forth over the crystal. She indicated that Ruby and I should do the same.

"I am going to give you a map to the stars, Lynn. You have lived your whole life just as we have lived ours, to experience this moment together."

Ruby nodded just as the heavy gold-gray mist floated in tendrils in and out of our circle. The movement of cool air shredded the mist into chiffon veils gently drifting overhead. Agnes and Ruby were intent on their crystals. Agnes would look directly at the jet sky and then shift her flashing crystal to another angle. I wondered what she was doing. Ruby was following Agnes.

"Lynn, hold your crystal at the base and do what I am doing," Agnes said. She got up and went toward the center of the circle. Ruby and I followed. Agnes very slowly turned her crystal in the starlight until I saw a needle of blue light. I exposed my crystal and tried to duplicate what Agnes had done. "Now catch the light of the star that you cannot see. The name of the star is Sirius. First find Venus." She pointed up through the parted mist to the inky sky. "Do you see it?"

I answered, "Yes." It was an icy chip in the cosmic ocean.

"Now, over there." I followed her direction. "Beyond that cluster is the home of Sirius, the medicine dog. Like your great Arion, he is the guardian of new worlds. Look into your crystal and catch his color. You will feel it. There will be a connection and the flame will leap. Watch the flame entity throw its breath out at you." She reached over and turned my crystal slightly in my hand. It caught the starlight and there was a rigadoon of fire.

"Good," Agnes said. "Visualize your central fire. Remember who you are. Lynn, realize that those stars out there are the sacred law belts surrounding your own center. Bring them in to you. You are their mother. They are your children waiting to be born. Listen for their voices. See their firelight in your hand."

Ruby and Agnes were now standing directly in front of me.

"Lynn," Ruby said, "the time has come to its end. Now is the time to awaken from the waking dream." Ruby moved her crystal in the starlight, and her whole body took on a red-tinged glow.

I moved my own crystal, and suddenly the flame inside caught a blue-green light that edged the flame in purple. The nature of the flame completely changed. It was no longer something removed from me. It had its own life, and the crystal disappeared or burned up. I was holding a tiny star in the palm of my hand with its center delicately flaming out toward me.

"Lynn," Agnes said, "be prepared for your journey. We will be with you."

"Don't be afraid," Ruby said. "We are leaving you for now." She looked at Agnes. "All my relations."

"All my ancestors," Agnes said.

There was an explosion of flame that sent out tongues of fire around both of them. I saw two round, flaming spheres where the two women had been standing.

"Ruby! Agnes!" I cried to the sheaths of fire.

I felt something break and a coolness surge up my arm. My terror was consumed by the flaming star in my hand. I saw two red lights going up in a perpendicular trajectory. The medicine circle had taken on a red glow, as had the red-tinged mist. The moon and the stars were spinning over me. I saw my arm was on fire.

"No!" I shouted, beating at the flame.

Across the circle there were tree stumps, broken and gnarled behind the swirls of fog. They were as skeletons from another age, reaching out with craggy branches as if to grasp a last taste of life.

I had managed to extinguish the flame crawling up my arm from the crystal. I was crying, tears streaming down my face. I felt as if I, too, were going to burst. Then I saw two blue-gray forms between the gnarled and jutting tree stumps that were projecting up from the ground. The earth was red and moving, as if everything solid were returning to a gaseous state. Hot and molten tendrils of steam were lifting off the surface and linking with the Milky Way, all smearing together in my vision. Then I looked down at the star flame in my hand. I realized the fire had crept up my arm again, all the way to my shoulder. There was no pain, save for a coldness and an excruciating pressure at the center of my soul. The power of the universe was imploding every cell of my body. I was being lifted and consumed by the stars.

The two shadowy forms moved closer. When they became distinguishable, I recognized their fiery eyes. They were two white horses with their legs edged in pink. Purple and green shadows surrounded their flanks and bellies. They came faster, straight toward me, breaking into a gallop.

A voice I had heard long ago spoke to me: "We are made from stars, and to the stars we must one day return."